PLAY SPACES
FOR CHILDREN:
A NEW BEGINNING
Improving Our
Elementary School Playgrounds

EDITOR:

Lawrence D. Bruya
North Texas State University

A project of the

American Alliance for Health, Physical Education, Recreation and Dance
American Association for Leisure and Recreation
Committee On Play

About the Alliance

The American Alliance for Health, Physical Education, Recreation, and Dance is an educational organization, structured for the purposes of supporting, encouraging, and providing assistance to member groups and their personnel throughout the nation as they seek to initiate, develop, and conduct programs in health, leisure, and movement-related activities for the enrichment of human life.

Alliance objectives included:

1.   Professional Growth and development- to support, encourage, and provide guidance in the development and conduct of programs in health, leisure, and movement-related activities which are based on the needs, interests, and inherent capacities of the individual in today's society.

2.   Communication- to facilitate public and professional understanding and appreciation of the importance and value of health, leisure, and movement-related activities as they contribute toward human well-being.

3.   Research- to encourage and facilitate research which will enrich the depth and scope of health, leisure, and movement-related activities; and to disseminate the findings to the profession and other interested and concerned publics.

4.   Standards and guidelines- to further the continuous development and evaluation of standards within the profession for personnel and programs in health, leisure, and movement-related activities.

5.   Public affairs- to coordinate and administer a planned program of professional, public, and governmental relations that will improve education in areas of health, leisure, and movement-related activites.

6.   To conduct such other activities as shall be approved by the Board of Governors and the Alliance Assembly, provided that the Alliance shall not engage in any activity which would be inconsistent with the status of an educational and charitable organization as defined in Section 501(c)(3) of the Internal Revenue Code of 1954 or any successor provision thereto, and none of the said purposes shall at any time be deemed or construed to be purposes other than the public benefits purposes and objectives consistent with such education and charitable status.

Bylaws, Article III

FOREWORD

To Advocate for Children and Their Playground

The group of professionals which eventually made up the Committee On Play consisted of a group of professionals dedicated to advocating for children and their right to play. During discussions which lead to the initiation of the National Survey of Elementary School Playground Equipment, other ideas also continued to be considered. Eventually, one of these was incorporated into the survey project concept and became the heart of the system to be used to advocate for children's play.

The idea for a collection of papers to describe a process to improve playgrounds grew from the report of the data and the information described in the survey (Bruya & Langendorfer, In Press). The text was to be a comprehendible series of ideas which could be used to initiate a plan of action designed to change the elementary school playgrounds. Fresh new works were collected. They reflect the most current thinking on the subject of playgrounds used in educational settings.

Diversity of Ideas

Nine professionals made contributions to this text. All papers were submitted to critical review. Although the ideas were varied and divergent at the onset they were thought to reflect a broad scope of information needed for adequately providing for the needs of children who play on elementary school plagrounds. As a unit they provide a base of information designed to reshape the ideas and the actions of the adults who are committed to the development of children's playspaces. Always, the intent was to provide information that could be used to advocate for children and their play.

The Review System

Reviewers were selected from professionals involved with children, professionals involved in design and professionals outside the process of this survey. The following includes all those who participated in the review process:

- Jay Beckwith; Playground Designer •
- Joe Frost; Early Childhood •
- Curt Fowler; Elementary School Teacher •
- Sharyl Green; Landscape Architect •
- Steven J. Langendorfer; Motor Development •
- Patty Lowe; Elementary School Teacher •
- Barbara Sampson; Recreation and Leisure •
- David Sommerfeld; Elementary School Administrator •
- Donna Thompson; Elementary Physical Education •
- Eileen Warrell; Elementary Physical Education •
- Sue Wortham; Early Childhood •

Contents

PART THREE :

Current Playground Solutions For Children

PART FOUR :

The School Playground and Risk

PART ONE:

The Rebirth of the American Playground

CHAPTER 1

CHILD DEVELOPMENT AND PLAYGROUNDS 1

by

Joe L. Frost
University of Texas

In order to understand and use the rapidly accumulating body of information about child development and its implications for children's playgrounds, one must place the relevant issues in historical perspective. Four major issues will be explored in this chapter: (1) theories and philosophies of play, (2) historical evolution of playgrounds, (3) research on child development, play and playgrounds, and (4) creating playgrounds that meet children's developmental needs.

Theories and Philosophies of Play

Historically, play has been regarded as wasteful, sinful, and frivilous and childhood often has been characterized by sexual abuse, infanticide, harsh discipline, and hard labor. Fortunately for children, a few philosophers and poets have been articulate in expressing their views of play. Plato and Aristotle agreed that children should engage in play and that play was a primary influence in the education of the young. From 1600 to the early 1900's,

Comenius, Locke, Luther, Basedow, Rousseau, Pestalozzi, Froebel, Dewey, Montessori, and Gesell all argued that play was important in the development of children and proposed its integration into educational programs. The views of these romanticists conflicted with the beliefs of the general populace during their respective periods and set them apart as liberal or radical.

Older Views of Play. With the onset of the scientific era, scholars began to complement the views of philosophers with the conclusions of "organized logic." The surplus energy theory, commonly expressed by educators as "the need to expend excess energy," can be traced to Aristotle, the poet Schiller in 1800, to Herbert Spencer's writing in 1875, and to Karl Groos (1898). In rapid succession the instinct-practice theory (Groos, 1898), the recapitulation theory (Gulick, 1920; Hall, 1906) and the relaxation theory (Patrick, 1916) were formulated. These theories implied narrow, insipid roles for children's play. The implications of these theories for playgrounds would focus upon space for motor activities and space for running off excess energy (surplus energy theory), practicing or repeating motor skills (instinct-practice theory), sand and water for digging, crawling and climbing (recapitulation theory), and space for running, throwing and climbing (relaxation theory).

Given this body of theory, it is little wonder that the earliest playgrounds were of such sterile design. The first American playground for young children, established in Boston in 1886, consisted essentially of heaps of sand, patterned after the sandgardens of Berlin (Sapora and Mitchell, 1948). Consistent with early theory emphasizing physical training and excess energy, the

4

earliest park playgrounds were called outdoor gymnasiums. They were equipped with exercise apparatus, tracks and space for games. Later, many schoolyard playgrounds followed this same pattern.

The 1928 National Recreation Association Guidelines proposed that preschool playgrounds contain a sand box, six chair swings, a small slide and a simple low climber (Butler, 1958). The elementary school playground should contain a horizontal ladder, a balance beam, a giant stride, six swings on a frame twelve feet high, a slide eight feet high with a chute sixteen feet long, a horizontal bar and optional equipment such as traveling rings, see-saws and low climbing devices. Equipment was to be made of galvanzied steel, swing seats of hardwood, slides narrow enough to ensure one at a time sliding with an eight inch platform at the top. The design and materials should ensure economical maintenance, simplicity of supervision, safety and recreational value (Butler, 1958).

These guidelines, consistent with the theories of the times, established patterns of playground design that continue to exert profound influence on today's playgrounds. All of the equipment described is still available from some of today's manufacturers! The general playground description could just as accurately be applied to most public schools today as it was sixty years ago! It is as though many manufacturers and consumers were in a time-warp, oblivious to the research and development of the past half century.

It is to the credit of early playground developers that the first guidelines for surfacing, developed by the National Recreation Association in 1932, recommended special resilent surfacing such as tanbark, sawdust, shavings, or sand under climbing, rotating, and

5

sliding equipment. Unfortunately, this recommendation, though reiterated in publications on playground safety over the past fifty years, has yet to be extensively implemented.

Fortunately, contemporary theories of play have the advantage of reflecting a growing body of scientific evidence. They expand the emphasis of early theories on exercise or motor activities to a broad complex of developmental benefits of play, including cognitive, social, emotional and perceptual-motor effects. As expected the more recent theories do focus upon the biases and expertise of their developers, but taken collectively the broad range of human development is considered (see Frost, 1985).

Recent Views of Play: Emotional, Cognitive, Social and Perceptual-Motor Bases. The psychoanalytic theory of play has roots in earlier cathartic theory which held that play was an activity for pursuing painful or pleasant feelings and emotions. This emphasis upon emotions and emotional development in play originated with Freud in the early 1900's and was elaborated by Walder (1933) and Erikson (1950). Freud (1959) believed that play revealed the inner life and motivation of the child and that play was a vehicle for reenacting unpleasant experiences and thus, mastering them. In so doing, the child develops control over his/her emotions and the need to play is reduced as he/she grows older.

Erikson added cognitive dimensions to Freud's emotional constructs, explaining the developmental progression of play and the resulting cognitive and emotional development from infancy to adulthood. In a manner similar to Piaget, he proposed an infancy period of exploratory play centered upon the infant's body,

6

accompanied by vocalizations (language development) and kinesthetic sensations. Through such play, the child develops new skills, leading to a second stage of learning to manage toys and objects and, finally, to a third stage where the child shares play with others.

These views of child development through play call for an expansion of the traditional playground to include a wider range of opportunities, places, and materials. The child needs semi-private harbors for overhauling or playing out shattered emotions; places for social play and learning, and for interacting and cooperating with others. The child also needs a wide range of movable materials (loose parts) for creating model situations, mastering emotions, and constructing reality by experiment and planning.

Erikson's view that the child achieves emotional, social, and intellectual mastery through play are basic elements in Piaget's cognitive-developmental theory. Piaget (1962) linked the developmental progression of play to his stages of cognitive development. Contrary to popular opinion, his descriptions of the progression of games (play) are not totally original, but draw from the earlier work of Charlotte Buhler (1935) and Karl Buhler (1937).

To Piaget, play is a vehicle for knowing, (i.e., learning and cognitive development) and, as such, is an indicator of the child's cognitive development. He views intelligence as the organization of adaptive behavior. Adaptation is the modification of the organism through organism-environment interchanges (which can occur during play). Consequently, opportunities for the child to interact with concrete objects are essential in his/her development. Adaptation occurs through the reciprocal processes of assimilation and accommodation. Assimilation is the action of the organism on objects; accommodation is the action of the environment on the organism. In play, reality (objects as symbols) is modeled or bent to the wishes of the child (assimilation). In imitation, the child adapts himself (cognitive structure) to reality, mimicking or accommodating to the actions of another person.

Processes of Play. The cognitive play categories initially proposed by Buhler and expanded by Piaget and numerous researchers are called by several names-practice, often referred to as functional or exercise, originates and dominates during infancy. Practice play is the repetition of actions already learned, followed by elaboration of themes in the presence of materials (toys) and frequently gaining language support from one or more adults. Some dimensions of the second category-dramatic, often referred to as imaginative, make believe, pretend, or symbolic, are clearly seen during infancy. Dramatic play emerges full bloom at about two years of age and involves the substitution of imaginary objects (mental imagery or symbolic behavior) for real objects, animals or people in make-believe play situations. A third category, construction or constructive is also seen evolving around age two. Children build or construct designs (bridges, houses, etc.) from simple materials (loose parts) such as blocks or tinker toys. At about age five years, games with rules and specific organization are emerging. Children begin to accept prearranged rules and adjust to them in their games shared with other children (hopscotch, jacks, football, etc.).

Parten (1932) is credited with categorizing social play. In solitary play the child plays alone and independently. In parallel play the child plays in close proximity to other children but not with them. In associative play, the child plays alternately with other children and alone but each child plays as he or she chooses. In cooperative play the child participates as a member of a cooperatively organized play group striving to attain a common goal.

These categorizations of cognitive and social play have endured the test of many research projects (e.g., Smilanski, 1968; Rubin, Maioni, and Hornung, 1976; Frost and Campbell, 1985; Henniger, 1985). With modifications for age groups and research contexts, remain viable systems for communicating about play. Indeed, these categories or processes of play appear to be viable across nations and cultures, that is, all normal (healthy) children engage in these play processes in a generally predictable manner. Babies in China or the United States engage in practice play; preschoolers in Africa and Australia engage in dramatic play; elementary school age children in England and Japan participate in organized games-and they do this without teaching or specific directions. Play is a natural phenomenon in human behavior. It is done by all healthy children and the patterns or processes of play are remarkably similar across geographical areas. However, it should be noted that the content (toys, imaginary models, equipment) of play differs markedly from culture to culture. For example, the symbolic content of American children's play is predominatly television characters, and their playthings are primarily manufactured dolls, wheeled vehicles, war toys, and manufactured swing/slide/climbing sets. Children's symbolic play in remote areas involves traditional mother/father and community member roles and their playthings are more natural (rocks, sticks, water, dirt) and self-made toys (dolls, weapons, etc.).

Developmental Benefits of Play. The common belief that play is a waste of time is perhaps the single most restrictive factor in providing good play environments. The contemporary elementary school playground is designed as though playground activity contributes nothing to thinking, relating, and creating. A second source of this problem appears to be the prevailing naivete` about the benefits of play among designers, teachers, administrators, parents, and politicians. A rapidly growing body of research data now provides overwhelming evidence of the multiple benefits of play for the overall development of children.

From a therapeutic perspective, play is a means for overcoming fears (Klein, 1932; Isaacs, 1933; Axline, 1947; Erikson, 1950). Play promotes cognitive development (Sutton-Smith, 1967, 1977; Piaget, 1962; Saltz and Brodie, 1982; Fein, 1979; Saltz, 1980; Bruner, 1972; Bruner, Jolly and Sylva, 1976). Play leads to discovery, verbal judgment and reasoning and it is important in developing manipulative skills, imaginative art, discovery, reasoning and thought (Isaacs, 1933). Play with objects results in divergent production or expands uses for objects (Sutton-Smith, 1968; Goodnow, 1969; Dansky, 1980b) and improves problem solving (Sylva, 1977; Smith and Dutton, 1979; Dansky and Silverman, 1973). Play is a necessary part of culture. Culture arises in the form of play (Huizinga, 1950).

Play training for children enhances imaginative play (Smilansky, 1968; Feitelson and Ross, 1973; Smith and Sydall, 1978), enhances creativity (Feitelson and Ross, 1973; Dansky, 1980a), enhances language development (Vygotsky, 1967; Lovinger, 1974; Saltz, Dixon and Johnson, 1977), and enhances group cooperation (Rosen, 1974; Smith and Sydall, 1978). Play training for teachers improves their interaction with children during play (Busse, Ree and Gutride, 1970; Wade, 1984).

It is anticipated that this growing body of evidence of the benefits of children's play and of the efficacy of educating teachers about play will lead to the introduction of new courses of study in institutions of higher education including schools of architecture education, child development and physical education. Awareness of this body of evidence should eventually lead to radical modification of thought and action in designing and using children's playgrounds.

Evolution of Playgrounds

Insofar as playground design is concerned, acceptance and understanding of the benefits of play have led some adults to develop creative places for children's play. Among the many types of playgrounds developed over the decades, most were hazardous and ill-suited to the developmental and learning needs of children. As we have seen, the traditional playground, originating around the turn of the present century, featured hazardous, heavy, fixed steel equipment of limited function, installed on hard surfaces which was poorly maintained and supervised. This traditional playground remains the dominant type for today's elementary schools. During

World War II and post war years (1950's and 1960's), theme equipment (steam engines, airplanes, mammoth insects, wild west villages, sculptured equipment (animals and abstract concrete and plastic forms) was popular along with concrete pipe creations. During the 1970's modular wood equipment featuring super-structures with multiple apparatuses for perceptual-motor development became popular. This was followed by the introduction in the early 1980's of modularized, powder coated steel and aluminum superstructures, also oriented to perceptual-motor development.

Playgrounds specifically designed to enhance creativity in children, are frequently called creative playgrounds. Research comparing play on creative versus traditional playgrounds shows that exercise play and organized games are significantly higher on the traditional playground and dramatic and construction play are significantly higher on the creative playground (Frost and Campbell, 1985; Campbell and Frost, 1984; Strickland, 1979). On a creative playground with a variety of loose parts, the children were the characters in dramatic play. On a traditional playground where loose parts were absent, the children merely talked out roles (Strickland, 1979). Children prefer action-oriented over static equipment (Frost and Campbell, 1985; Campbell and Frost, 1985). Play and safety are enhanced by the addition of sand underneath structures (Frost and Klein, 1983), variety in play behaviors is stimulated (Bowers, 1976) and time at play and peer interaction are increased (Bruya, 1985).

Superstructure value is enhanced further by providing loose parts to use under and around the superstructure for dramatic and constructive play (Frost and Klein, 1983; Strickland, 1979). Loose parts provide for flexibility, diversity, novelty, and challenge which are all important ingredients for creativity, socialization, and learning. They also are adaptable for use with fluid materials (sand and water) and with larger structures (Strickland, 1979; Noren-Bjorn, 1982).

Overall, the research shows that traditional playgrounds are poor play spaces from both safety and developmental perspectives (Hole, 1966). They fail in terms of use rates when compared to alternate play spaces such as vacant lots and roads not designed for play (Holme and Massey, 1971) and they have lower attendance rates, compared to creative playgrounds (Frost and Strickland, 1978) and compared to adventure playgrounds (Hayward, Rothenberg & Beasley 1974).

Adventure Playgrounds

In the context of this review of research on child development, play, and playgrounds, an inescapable conclusion emerges. For enhancing the total development of children, adventure playgrounds are head and shoulders above most others in quality and range of opportunities for children. The adventure playground concept originated in Denmark and proliferated in other European countries. The jury is still out on the safety of adventure playgrounds. Undoubtedly, play leaders are a key factor in promoting safety on any playground.

It is interesting, indeed, that the best playgrounds for children did not emerge from research but originated in the creative genius and concern of a few play environment pioneers. Little did C. Th. Sorensen realize in 1943, upon establishing the first "waste material playground" (Lady Allen of Hurtwood, 1968) in Emdrup, Denmark, that his creation would usher in a new era in playgrounds. His simple aim, ". . . to give children in towns the same chance for creative play as those in the country. . ." could not have been more consistent with accepted principles of child development. Sorensen and his followers understood that children need opportunities to create for themselves, that their play is infinitely varied, and that play opportunities must also be infinitely varied.

Sorensen's ideas for "junk" playgrounds came from his sensitive observations of children playing on construction sites with scraps of materials and the terrain itself. He understood that modern civilization hampered the play of children with hygenic, overstructured, adult inspired playgrounds, so he provided tools, materials and space and allowed children to build, change and create, for themselves.

Another primary factor in the success of adventure playgrounds was the success of the first play leader, John Bertlesen (Lambert, 1974). Abernethy (1968) described the ideal leader as a combination of mother and father, policeman, and Robin Hood. Lambert (1974), a play leader himself, said of the play leader, "He is the touchstone on which they will return in moments of excitement and moments of crisis."

The adventure play concept has gradually expanded across much of Europe. Bengtsson (1973) credited Sorensen with the concept, Bertlesen with the philosophy and Lady Allen of Hurtwood with telling the world about it. Indeed, Lady Allen was responsible for the British adventure playground movement. She established the first adventure playgrounds for handicapped children in London and, in 1966, formed the Handicapped Adventure Playground Association.

In contrast to the traditional American playground, the adventure playground allows children to create the form and structure of their own play rather than have it imposed by an unmalleable environment. The London Adventure Playground Association (Jago, 1971) described adventure playgrounds:

> An adventure playground can best be described as a place where children are free to do many things that they cannot easily do elsewhere in our crowded urban society. In an adventure playground, which can be any size from one third of an acre to two and a half acres, they can build houses, dens and climbing structures with waste materials, have bonfires, cook in the open, dig holes, garden, or just play with sand, water and clay. The atmosphere is permissive and free, and this is especially attractive to children whose lives are otherwise much limited and restricted by lack of space and opportunities.
> Each playground has two full-time leaders in charge who are friends to the children, and help them with what they are trying to do. There is a large hut on each playground and this is well equipped with materials for painting, dressing up and acting, modeling and other forms of indoor play. There are also a record player, table tennis and so on, so that in bad weather and in winter the adventure playground hut becomes a social center for many children who would have nowhere to play except the street.

In the best adventure playgrounds of Denmark and Sweden, additional features are seen. In Stockholm the author observed a group of children assisting a sow in giving birth to pigs. Others worked in gardens with their grandparents and still others socialized in a canteen-like area featuring food, drinks, and games for the children. In Copenhagen one group of children fed and brushed the horses, cleaned the stables, and later prepared the horses for riding. In another playground children constructed hutches for their rabbits and fed their chickens. And on a third, children prepared outdoor fires in the area designed for that purpose and set about to cook their evening meal. All of this occurred with the unobtrusive involvement of play leaders. Construction areas (building areas), storage bins and buildings, under-fire's areas, gardens, animal hutches, cooking areas, wading pools, sand areas, climbing structures, commons areas (organized games) and main buildings (indoor recreation) are all common features of adventure playgrounds.

The adventure playground is indeed consistent with the philosophies of many noted philosopher-educators: Dewey - children learn through experience; Piaget - children learn through actions on concrete objects; Keats - "Nothing ever becomes real until it is experienced."; Whitehead - "From the very beginning of his education the child should experience the joy of discovery."; Schiller - "As for art, so for play, freedom is entirely necessary." The defense for adventure playgrounds then, makes up in philosophy what it lacks in research.

Unfortunately for children the history of success for adventure playgrounds in Europe has had limited influence on American playgrounds. Slowness of acceptance in the United States is due to a combination of factors including objection to their untidy appearance, ignorance about the nature and importance of children's play, and unsubstantiated fears of injury and liability.

Creating Playgrounds that Meet Children's Developmental Needs

Given these positive views of adventure playgrounds a logical conclusion could well be, "If one wishes to create developmentally appropriate play spaces for children, then one should go out and build adventure playgrounds." Indeed, such a movement would lead to dramatic improvements over conventional American playgrounds. But the relevant conclusion is not what type of playgrounds to build or even by what name they should be called but what should playgrounds be like if they are to be developmentally appropriate for children?

There is a striking contrast between developmentally appropriate playgrounds and typical American elementary school playgrounds. The results of the National Elementary School Playground Equipment Survey show that the ten most common types of equipment are: chinning bars (16% of all equipment), swings (13%), overhead ladders (10%), flat slides (9%), fireman's pole (9%), balance beams (8%), monkey bars (8%), see-saws (6%), parallel bars (5%), geodesic domes (3.5%). Sand play containers were 1.3% of all equipment and water play containers comprised 1%. Half of the playgrounds had hard surfaces that would accommodate wheeled vehicles but the survey did not determine whether wheeled vehicles were available. Smaller sized play equipment for younger children was present in 64% of the playgrounds (Bruya & Langendorfer, In Press).

Overall the results reveal that elementary school playgrounds are much like those of a half-century ago and they are still in general compliance with the National Recreation Association's 1928 guidelines! The typical playground contains an array of equipment designed to facilitate motor development without regard to social, emotional and cognitive development and emphasizes exercise play, with little equipment appropriate to dramatic and construction play. With respect to the issue, "Is the contemporary elementary school playground appropriate to the developmental needs of children?" one can charitably assign a grade of D-. When the overall findings of the survey, including safety data, are considered the grade must be reduced. A large number of hazards were reported, including hard surfaces under equipment, exposed concrete footings, heavy metal and wood swing seats, sharp corners and projections, broken and missing parts, excessive climbing heights, entrapment areas, and shearing or crushing areas on rotating devices.

The logical conclusion arising from studies using cognitive and social play categories is that the developmentally oriented playground should include space, materials, equipment and activities to enhance, enrich, and encourage all the forms or processes of play appropriate to the age or developmental levels of the children involved. For instance the play environment for infants should emphasize age/size appropriate equipment for motor development-climbing, swinging, sliding, crawling, etc.; loose parts for preliminary exploration behaviors - feeling, stacking, throwing, etc.; and simple toys (dolls, animals, etc.) for preliminary dramatic play behaviors. Obviously the play space for infants would not need a level, grassy field for organized games as would the playground for school age children.

By the time most children enter elementary school (kindergarten or first grade at age five or six) they are competent to engage in all of the major forms of play, both cognitive (exercise, dramatic, constructive, organized games) and social (solitary, parallel, associative, cooperative).

Consequently, the developmentally appropriate play environment should include materials, equipment, space and activities to enhance all forms of play. Elementary school playgrounds should be much larger than infancy/toddler and preschool playgrounds to accommodate the wider range of play engaged in by the older children. The range of loose parts and large equipment also would be more extensive.

Preschool (ages 3-5) and primary school (ages 5-9 or K-3) playgrounds should contain equipment designed primarily for exercise play (climbing, swinging, crawling, balancing, rotating, sliding, etc.); loose parts for dramatic and construction play (blocks, sand, water, sand and water play equipment, work benches with vices, garden tools, carpentry and mechanical tools, assorted tires and boards, etc.); a convenient storage facility linked to a wheeled vehicle track to house loose parts and wheeled vehicles; a large, flat grassy area for organized games, complemented with games materials (balls, bats, jump ropes, games, etc.) in the storage facility; semi-private areas to accommodate solitary and parallel play and to complement the organized games areas designed for cooperative organized play.

Because of the crowded conditions in urban areas and the large amount of time spent in school and watching television, schools now must assume responsibility for providing nature experiences for children that will enrich understandings and appreciation for the natural habitat and complement science teaching in the classroom. Nature areas should be provided in the play environment that allow children to observe, explore, experiment and play in an environment of plants, animals and natural terrain (hills, streams, rocks, etc.). Tools should be available for the children to use in caring for the total play environment and to help ensure sense of ownership and responsibility and to develop tool-using capabilities. Children also should have access to building and digging areas where they can learn to use tools (with supervision) in reconstructing the terrain, and in creating play houses and habitats for animals.

Modern superstructures provide within limited space, a broader array of exercise opportunities than did the traditional, single, or limited function equipment, scattered randomly or in rows about a playing field. The physical design of superstructures make it easier to provide a resilient surface in fall zones. But more importantly, superstructures enhance playability in five important ways: (1) the sand used for fall zones is also a medium for children's dramatic and construction play; (2) virtually unlimited complexity and perceptual-motor opportunities (gross motor, fine motor, body awareness, spatial awareness, directional awareness, balance activities, expressive activities, integration activities) can be

ntegrated into the modular structures; (3) the provision of loose
parts in rich variety can further enhance various forms of social,
cognitive and motor play; (4) the structures themselves can be
designed to create semi-private places (under decks) for children's
play; (5) superstructures feature linkage between activity options
that lead children from activity to activity and these activity options
challenges) can be moved from place to place on the superstructure.
Overall, the modern modular superstructures, when properly
designed and complemented with sand, loose parts, materials for
building and natural terrain for interacting with nature, represent a
giant step forward in play structure development. The writer
anticipates that a next major step by designers will be to increase
flexibility by making structures free-standing rather than setting
them in concrete.

The growing body of evidence (Frost, 1986) points to a play
environment containing complex superstructures and simple loose
parts to be used in combination. The apparent contradiction is
resolved when one considers that large, complex structures cannot
readily be modified by children. Thus, complexity must be built in.
On the other hand, children can create with loose parts in almost
unlimited fashion. Since children create characters through mental
imagery the loose parts need not be theme specific - raw materials
such as water, sand, lumber, tires, spools, etc. function very
effectively.

Finally, everyone concerned with children's playgrounds must
grow to understand that traditional American playgrounds are
inappropriate from both safety and developmental perspectives.

Public school administrators and teachers receive little or no formal training about play and child development and hold play in low regard. School boards, seeing little support for play in the schools, leave playground development to parent-teacher organizations and channel public funds to academics and organized sports. It is hoped that the rapidly growing body of research evidence for the value of children's play will lead to changed attitudes and improved playgrounds.

End Notes

1. Presented at the National Convention of the American Alliance for Health, Physical Education, Recreation and Dance, Las Vegas, Nevada, April 13, 1987.

References

Abernethy, D. (1968). Play leadership. London: National Playing Fields Association.

Allen, Lady of Hurtwood (1968). Planning for play. Cambridge: MIT Press.

Axline, V. (1947). Play therapy. Boston: Houghton Mifflin.

Bengtsson, A. (1973). Adventure playgrounds. New York: Praeger.

Bowers, L. (1976). Play learning centers for pre-school handicapped children. Tampa, FL: University of South Florida.

Bruner, J. S. (1972). The nature and uses of immaturity. American Psychologist, 27, 687-708.

Bruner, J. S., Jolly, A., & Sylva, K. (Eds.) (1976). Play: Its role in development and evolution. New York: Penguin.

Bruya, L. D. (1985). The effect of play structure format differences on the play behavior of preschool children. In J. L. Frost (Ed.), When children play. Washington, DC: Association for Childhood Education International.

Bruya, L. D. & Langendorger, S. J. (Eds.). (In Press). *Where our children play: Elementary school playgrounds.* Washington, DC: AAHPERD, AALR-COP.

Buhler, C. (1935). From birth to maturity. London: Routledge & Kegan Paul.

Buhler, K. (1937). The mental development of the child. London: Routledge & Kegan Paul.

Busse, T., Ree, M., & Gutride, M. (1970). Environmentally enriched classrooms and the play behavior of Negro preschool children. Urban Education, 5, 128-140.

Butler, G. D. (1958). <u>Recreation areas: Their design and equipment</u> (2nd ed.). New York: The Ronald Press.

Campbell, S., & Frost, J. L. (1985). The effects of playground type on the cognitive and social play behavior of grade two children. In J. L. Frost (Ed.), <u>When children play</u>. Washington, DC: Association for Childhood Education International.

Dansky, J. L., & Silverman, I. W. (1973). Effects of play on associative fluency in preschool-aged children. <u>Developmental Psychology, 9</u>, 38-43.

Dansky, J. L. (1980a). Cognitive consequences of sociodramatic play and exploratory training for economically disadvantaged preschoolers. <u>Journal of Child Psychology and Psychiatry, 20</u>, 47-58.

Dansky, J. L. (1980b). Make believe: A mediator of the relationship between free play and associative fluency. <u>Child Development, 51</u>, 576-579.

Erikson, E. H. (1950). <u>Childhood and society</u>. New York: Norton.

Fein, G. (1979). Play in the acquisition of symbols. In L. Katz (Ed.), <u>Current topics in early childhood education</u>. Norwood, NJ: Ablex.

Feitelson, W., & Ross, G. S. (1973). The neglected factor--play. <u>Human Development, 16</u>, 202-223.

Freud, S. (1959). Beyond the pleasure principle. In J. Strachey (Ed.), <u>The standard edition of the complete psychological works of Sigmund Freud</u>. London: The Institute of Psychoanalysis. (Original work published 1922).

Frost, J. L. (1985). <u>Toward an integrated theory of play: The young child and music</u>. Wheaton, MD: Association for Childhood Education International.

Frost, J. L. (1986). Children's playgrounds: Research and practice. In G. Fein (Ed.), <u>Play</u>. Washington, DC: National Association for the Education of Young Children.

Frost, J. L., & Campbell, S. (1985). Equipment choices of primary age children on conventional and creative playgrounds. In J. L. Frost & S. Sunderlin (Eds.), When children play. Wheaton, MD: Association for Childhood Education International.

Frost, J. L., & Klein, B. L. (1979). Children's play and playgrounds. Austin, TX: Playgrounds International.

Goodnow, J. J. (1969). Effects of handling, illustrated by use of objects. Child Development, 40, 201-212.

Groos, Karl. (1898). The play of animals. New York: D. Appleton.

Gulick, L. H. (1920). A philosophy of play. Washington, DC: McGrath.

Hall, G. S. (1906). Youth. New York: D. Appleton.

Hayward, D., Rothenberg, M., & Beasley, R. (1974). Children's play and urban playground environments: A comparison of traditional, contemporary and adventure playground types. Environment and Behavior,6(2), 131-168.

Henninger, M. (1985). Free play behaviors of nursery school children in an indoor and outdoor environment. In J. L. Frost & S. Sunderlin (Eds.), When children play. Wheaton, MD: Association for Childhood Education International.

Hole, V. (1966). Children's play on housing estates. London: HMSO.

Holme, A., & Masie. D. (1971). Children's play: A study of needs and opportunities. London: Michael Joseph.

Huizinga, J. (1950). Homo ludens: A study of the play element in culture. London: Routledge & Kegan Paul.

Isaacs, S. (1933). Social development in young children: A study of beginnings. London: Routledge & Kegan Paul.

Jago, L. (1971). Learning through experience. London: London Adventure Playground Association.

Klein, M. (1932). The psychoanalysis of children. London: Hogarth.

Lambert, J. (1974). Adventure playgrounds. New York: Praeger

Lovinger, S. L. (1974). Sociodramatic play and language development in preschool disadvantaged children. Psychology in the Schools, 11, 313-320.

Noren-Bjorn, E. (1982). The impossible playground. West Point, NY: Leisure Press (P. O. Box 3).

Parten, M. (1932). Social paticipation among preschool children. Journal of Abnormal and Social Psychology, 27, 243-269.

Patrick, G. T. W. (1916). The psychology of relations. New York: Houghton-Mifflin.

Piaget, J. (1962). Play, dreams and imitation in childhood. New York: W. W. Norton.

Rosen, C. E. (1974). The effects of sociodramatic play on problem solving among culturally disadvantaged children. Child Development, 45, 920-927.

Rubin, K. H., Maioni, T. L., & Hornung, M. (1976). Free play behaviors in middle- and lower-class preschoolers: Parten and Piaget revisited. Child Development, 47, 414-419.

Saltz, E. (1980). Pretend play: A complex of variables influencing development. Paper presented at the Annual Meeting of the American Psychological Association.

Saltz, E., & Brodie, J. (1982). Pretend-play training in childhood: A review and critique. In D. J. Pepler & K. H. Rubin (Eds.), The play of children: Current theory and practice. New York: S. Karger.

Saltz, E., Dixon, D., & Johnson, J. (1977). Training disadvantaged preschoolers on various fantasy activities: Effects on cognitive functioning and impulse control. Child Development, 48, 367-368.

Sapora, A., & Mitchell, E. D. (1948). The theory of play and recreation. New York: Ronald Press.

Singer, J., & Singer, D. (1974). Fostering imaginative play in preschool children: Effects of television viewing and direct adult modeling. Paper presented at the annual meeting of the American Psychological Association, New Orleans. (ERIC Document Reproduction Service No. 089 873).

Smilanski, S. (1968). The effects of sociodramatic play on disadvantaged preschool children. New York: John Wiley.

Smith, P. K., & Syddall, S. (1978). Play and non-play tutoring in preschool children: Is it play or tutoring which maters? British Journal of Education Psychology, 48, 315-325.

Smith, P. K., & Dutton, S. (1979). Play and training in direct and innovative problem solving. Child Development, 50, 830-836.

Strickland, E. V. (1979). Free play behaviors and equipment choices of third grade children in contrasting play environments. Unpublished doctoral dissertation, The University of Texas at Austin.

Sutton-Smith, B. (1977). Play as adaptive potentiation. In P. Stevens (Ed.), Studies in the anthropology of play. Cornwall, NY: Leisure Press.

Sutton-Smith, B. (1967). The role of play in child development. Young Children, 22, 361-370.

Sutton-Smith, B. (1968). Novel responses to toys. Merrill-Palmer Quarterly, 14, 151-158.

Sylva, K. (1977). Play and learning. In B. Tizard & D. Harvey (Eds.), Biology of play. London: Heineman.

Vygotsky, L. S. (1967). Play and its role in the mental development of the child. Soviet Psychology, 12, 62-76.

Wade, C. (1985). Effects of teacher training on teachers and children in playground settings. In J. Frost (Ed.), <u>When children play</u>. Washington, DC: Association for Childhood Education International.

Walder, R. (1933). The psychoanalytic theory of play. <u>Psychoanalytic Quarterly</u>, <u>2</u>, 208-224.

CHAPTER 2

PLAYGROUND DESIGN:
A SCIENTIFIC APPROACH *

by

L. Bowers
University of South Florida

The play of children is universally characterized by spontaneity, freedom, creativity, discovery, and joy (Herron & Sutton-Smith, 1971; Page, 1976; Noren-Bjorn, 1982). It can be observed that young children do not wait for a specified time to play, but at every opportunity initiate voluntary play activities as an important part of experiencing and discovering life. The play and development of children form an integral process through which self is explored in relationship to the world (see Figure 1).

Play takes many forms in making its contributions to the physical, psychological, and social development of children. Its most obvious form is the readily observable movement of children engaged in play. Young children both desire and need to involve their bodies in activities requiring forceful contraction of the muscles in order to promote growth and maintain the size and strength of both the muscular and skeletal systems. In addition,

* This paper has been developed from one which appeared in October of 1979 in the Leisure Today Section of JOHPERD and in the separate Leisure Today suppliment Edited by J. Levey, Oct, 1970, 21-24.

the growing child also requires sensory-motor experiences for the achievement of control and coordination of movements of the body. Physical activity in which the body is moved up, over, down, under, and through a variety of environmental challenges is both necessary for and enjoyable to the young child. Thus, basic movements such as rolling, crawling, climbing, walking, jumping, leaping, running and sliding are natural and important expressions in the natural play of children (Roberton and Halverson, 1984).

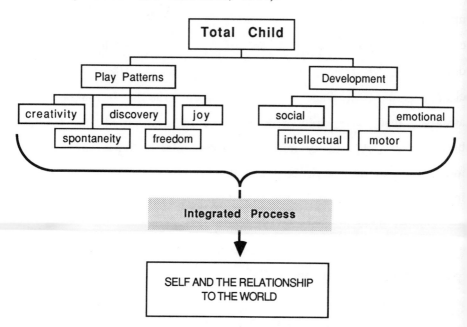

Figure 2.1 The play process and normal development interact during the early years of life to provide information about the childs' place in the world.

The play of children in its natural form is readily expressed in an accessible play space which has grass, uneven terrain, climbing trees, sand, water and materials for building. However, with a continuing increase in human population these play spaces are being replaced by buildings, parking lots, housing developments, and agriculture. In an effort to substitute for the vanishing natural play areas, parks, schoolgrounds, and backyards have been designated as the outdoor places in which children should play. Isolated, traditional swings, see saws, slides, merry-go-rounds and monkey bars have been designed by adults to provide variety within these often-barren, reclaimed play spaces.

If play equipment is to serve the needs for play of children, it must accommodate all players (see Figure 2.2). This includes young children with limited control of movements, children with varying degrees of physical and/or mental impairment, and able bodied children with high levels of movement capabilities. Currently, there are over seven million school-aged children in the United States who, because of an impairment or lack of development of the skeletal, muscular or nervous systems, are classified as physically, intellectually, or emotionally handicapped.

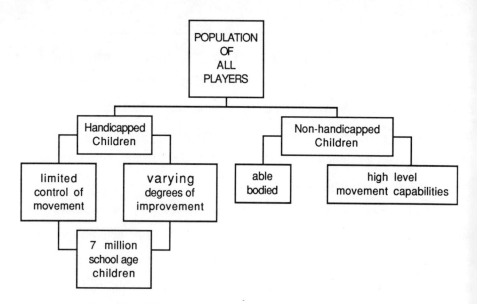

Figure 2.2 Play grounds must serve the needs of all children.

While the rate of development of basic movement ability in these children is usually slower than that of the non-handicapped child, the sequence and pattern of motor development is basically the same for both groups of children. Furthermore, the results of a study completed by Bowers (1977) indicated that, when provided accessible and safe play equipment, handicapped children select play activities similiar to that of a group of non-handicapped children matched for age and sex as they engaged in play in the same play environment (see Figure 2.3).

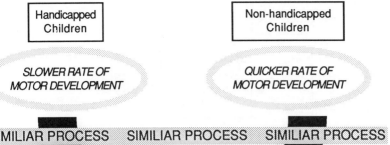

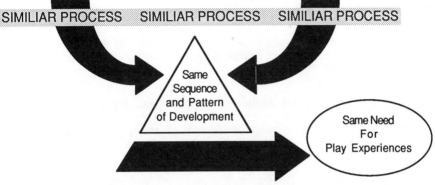

Figure 2.3   The motor development of a handicapped person is basically the same
as the development of the non-handicapped person except at a slower
rate.

The natural play of all children which is characterized by
xploration, creativity, and gaining mastery over new physical
hallenges is in direct conflict with the limited ways in which
raditional play equipment can be used.   Play equipment that allows
nly one child at a time to climb, slide, or swing in a singular
rescribed way severely limits the imaginative play of children (see
igure 2.4).

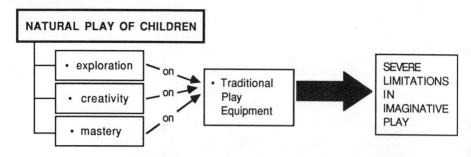

Figure 2.4 Equipment designed to be used in a single manner by the children who use them cannot meet a player's need for variation, thus thwarting imaginative play.

Whenever the natural exploratory play behavior of children is in conflict with the single-standard design of the play equipment, the behavior is deemed inappropriate and thus the cause of an accident that may occur. A U.S. Consumer Product Safety Commission Report (1975) indicates that during the year 1974, approximately 118,000 persons in the United States received hospital emergency room treatment for injuries related to playground equipment. Over three-fourths of the reported injuries involved children under ten years of age.

A University of Iowa Playground Accident Report (1973) further indicated that less than half of an investigated number of playground accidents resulted from poor construction or inadequate maintenance. The remainder of the accidents was attributed to inappropriate use of equipment. The assumption that children play inappropriately on playground equipment seems far from being correct. The more likely explanation is that something is drastically wrong with the design of the play equipment since it appears to be inappropriate to the play needs of children. Could it be that the design of traditional play equipment is inappropriate for the natural play behavior of children?

There are alternatives! We can redesign the playground. Play equipment should be as varied and innovative as the children who use it. To provide variation and the opportunity for creative use, the designers and purchasers of play equipment now have information to support several empirically sound basic principles for play equipment design. If followed carefully during the design and construction of a playground, these principles support the development and the natural play of children.

Design Principle #1: Accessible to All Children

Play spaces should be located in those places in the community where children naturally play. Within those areas selected for play, the equipment should be accessible to all children. Accessibility means that the equipment is both safe and easy to get to, and once on the equipment, it is easy for a child to play independently and safely (see Figure 2.5). The equipment must accomodate very young children who are barely walking, as well as other slightly older children who are not yet sure of their movements. There must also be physical challenges within the play environment which will provide the higher performing child the opportunity to develop additional play capabilities.

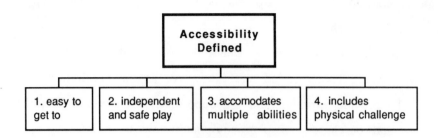

Figure 2.5 Accessibility on the play structure includes four distinctly different concepts for children's play.

There are also those children who because of physical or mental impairments do not demonstrate those performance levels in keeping with their chronological age. Thus, children of differing ages, physical size, and abilities have special needs which must be accomodated in the design of the play center. Gently sloping ramps, stairs with handrails, and platforms of gradually increasing heights are a few of the built-in enablers which provide for easier accessibility for all children (see Figure 2.6).

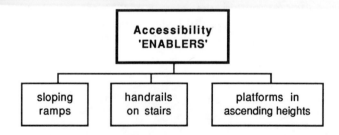

Figure 2.6 There are three important built-in accessibility enablers which designers can include in designs for children's play structures.

Accessibility of play equipment for all children has gained additional attention and importance as a design principle since Public

Law 94—142, the Education for the Handicapped Act, mandates accessibility for handicapped students in both academic and non-academic settings. Additional legislation in the form of the Rehabilitation Act of 1973 further requires that all public facilities be accessible for handicapped as well as non-handicapped persons.

Design Principle #2:   Safe Distance Between Levels

Children enjoy the challenge of climbing to the top of the hill or to the highest point on the playground. However, three-fourths of all playground injuries reported by the U.S. Consumer Product safety Commission (1975) were caused by falls to the ground or on other equipment. Providing a softer landing surface will reduce the seriousness of the injury sustained by a child in a fall to the ground. In addition the design of the play structure must preclude any possibility of a child falling from a high level (see Figure 2.7).

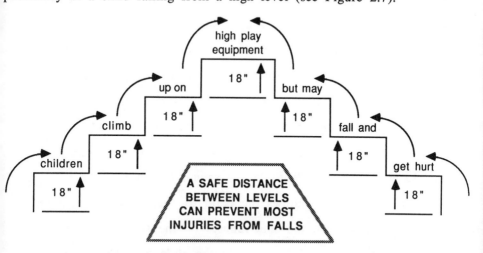

Figure 2.7 A safe distance between levels of a structure can prevent serious injury should a fall occur.

While relatively high levels to climb up to or slide down from may need to be part of the overall design, each level adjacent to the next highest level should be a reasonably safe distance. A safe distance between levels is one in which each child is able to jump purposely or fall accidental to the next level without sustaining a serious injury. For preschool age children a distance of 18 inches between levels is reasonable (Bowers, 1977). This multi-level design principle not only contributes to safety from falling, but greatly enhances accessibility to the higher levels of the play apparatus.

Design Principle #3: Variety of Inclines

Inclines should range from gently sloping angles to angles of not more than 45 degrees. There should be a variety of inclines of increasing challenge which will invite children to crawl, climb, run and/or slide according to the present level of ability of each child. Ramps with handrails, flat surface inclines, stairs, and wide climbing nets are a few of the types of inclines which give children a choice in moving up to and down from various levels of the play equipment.

When an inclined platform with a flat surface is placed on an angle it becomes a sliding surface (see Thompson, In Press). Flat slides should be wide enough to accomodate sliding by more than one child at a time (see Photo 1) and should be placed at an appropriate angle which allows the child to control his/her rate of descent. In addition to the side runners on the sliding surface, there should be horizontal platforms next to the slide to minimize the distance of a possible fall (see Photo 2). Full and half-circle tube

lides provide an added degree of safety and provide a different
liding experience for players (see Photo 3 & 4).

Photo 1	Photo 2	Photo 3	Photo 4
Double-wide slide.	Platforms near slide.	Tube slide.	Half slides.

Design Principle #4: Partially-closed Spaces

Children enjoy playing in partially-enclosed spaces, but these
spaces must be easy to get into and out of safely. This private space
should be shaded , should encourage quiet imaginative play, and also
should support role playing as a part of the total play experience.
These partially-enclosed play spaces can easily serve as connecting
links between play areas . The overall design of the
play apparatus should be abstract enough so that the creativity of
the child can make it into many imagined places (see Photo 5). It is
more difficult to think of a play structure as being something else if
it is constructed in the shape of a fire engine or train.

39

Photo 5 Abstract play apparatus.

Design Principle #5:   Complex and Stimulating

The best assessment of any play equipment is the amount and quality of continued play freely engaged in by the children for which it was designed.   It is also reasonable to assume that a play environment with a high degree of complexity would result in a greater amount of use by children for play than a simple play environment (Fowler, 1981).   Variations in color, texture and type of material are easily observable complexity variables (Farnham-Diggory & Gregg, 1975; Williams, 1983).

Perhaps the most important contribution to the concept of complexity on the play structure is the variation in the size and the shape of the physical structure itself.   A design which challenges the child to process new sensory information with every movement and to respond appropriately to maintain or to develop mastery over the environment may well provide the most interest and challenge for

he child. Ideally, if modular components of the play center can be
ppropriately rearranged, a new play environment can periodically
e created (see Figure 2.8).

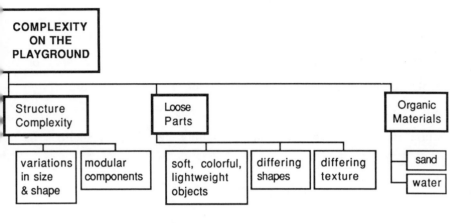

Figure 2.8 Structural complexity and loose parts can be designed as a part of
the play center to increase the amount and quality of time the
player will continue to play.

Nicholson's Theory of Loose Parts (1971) stresses the
mportance of having movable pieces within the play center which
an be manipulated by the players. Soft, colorful, lightweight objects
f different shapes and textures as well as organic material like sand
nd water for pouring and shaping all add complexity to the play
xperience (see Figure 2.8).

Bowers (1977) reported that when large foam blocks and large,
oft playground balls were introduced to preschool handicapped
hildren who had engaged in thirty-one half-hour periods of
nstructured play there was a substantial increase in the recorded
lay behavior of the children. There was both an increase in the
lay behaviors involving movements on the equipment in the play

41

center as well as increases in the manipulative activities with the blocks and the balls.

Design Principle #6:   Interconnected Play Areas

An interconnected play area is one in which easy movement throughout the play structure is developed through the inclusion of alternate routes of travel.   An overview of the play structure design should demonstrate easily accessed variations to parts of the play structure through pathways, ramps, climbing nets, stairs, inclines or slides (see Figure 2.9).

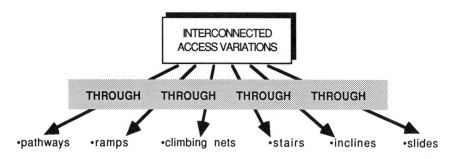

Figure   2.9 Access variations can be used to create interconnections.

Shaw (1976) investigated interconnections between parts of the structure which he came to call the "Unified Play Structure." As a result of the Creative Learning Project, he determined that overall use patterns decreased for separated play modules when compared to the "unified" play space. Thus, by unifying or interconnecting play elements in a play space, overall complexity was increased (see Figure 2.10).

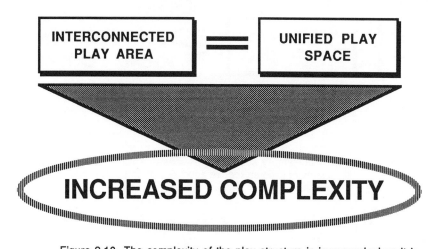

Figure 2.10 The complexity of the play structure is increased when it is interconnected or unified during the design process.

Design Principle # 7: Strong Materials - Quality Construction

To insure a developmentally sound interconnected play areas for children, strong materials which are non-toxic, durable and appropriate to the climatic conditions of the region should be used. It is necessary that design work which meets the need for integrated but spontaneous and natural play of children be supported with high-grade construction materials (see Figure 2.11). In this way a good play structure has a chance to meet the demands of the children who play on it as well as the needs of administrators who provide support processes for maintenance of the structure.

GOOD DESIGN	+	HIGHGRADE MATERIALS	=	DEVELOPMENTALLY SOUND PLAY AREA

- Non-toxic
- Durable
- Appropriate to Climatic Conditions

Figure 2.11 Developmentally sound Play structures which support the play patterns of children require good design and high-grade materials.

As a complement to the use of high-grade materials, the process designed to insure quality construction is also important. Appropriate construction procedures are evident in the elimination of sharp corners, splinters, small openings, and protruding bolts. Through concern for quality and an inspection process designed to insure competent construction, a play center is developed which will withstand the dynamic forces generated by the active play of the young children who use it as well as older and heavier children and adults (see Figure 2.12).

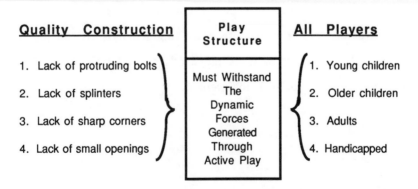

Quality Construction

1. Lack of protruding bolts
2. Lack of splinters
3. Lack of sharp corners
4. Lack of small openings

Play Structure

Must Withstand The Dynamic Forces Generated Through Active Play

All Players

1. Young children
2. Older children
3. Adults
4. Handicapped

Figure 2.12 Quality construction is necessary if the structure is to withstand the dynamic forces of all players likely to use it.

Conclusion

A well designed play center should utilize and enhance the natural environment surrounding it, should be accessible to all children, and should increase both the amount, variety and safety of play opportunities for children (see Figure 2.13). The current trend in the playground equipment industry away from traditional pieces of play equipment to interconnected units of equipment is a positive sign. Morover, the design and research efforts of a number of individual designers may be the beginning of the elevation of the design of play equipment to a science.

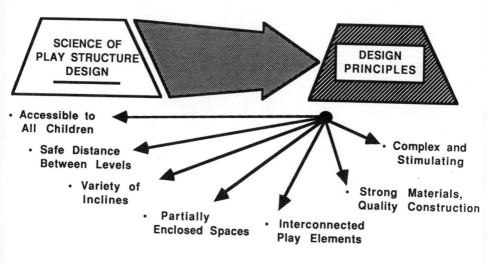

Figure 2.13 The science of play structure design must be based on principles which have been experimentally and field tested.

The players who use the play structures in schools are usually young developing children who may be physically impaired. Understanding the importance of routinely considering the importance of play centers which support a developmental notion of play, the need for understanding the ways in which children naturally play, and consideration of the special needs of children due to physical, intellectual or emotional impairment is long overdue. The science of play structure design is now possible and is badly needed.

Bibliography

Bowers, L. (August, 1977). Play Learning Centers for Preschool Handicapped Children (U.S.O.E.. Research and Demonstration Project Report). Tampa, Florida: College of Education, University of South Florida.

Farnham-Diggory, S., & Gregg, L. (1975). Color form and function as dimensions of natural classification: Developmental changes in eye movements, reaction time and response strategies. Child Development, 46, pp.101-114.

Fowler, C. (1983). The effects of complexity on play equipment usage of three-, four-, and five-year-old children. Denton, Texas: Unpublished Master's Thesis, North Texas State University.

Herron, R. E., & Sutton-Smith, B. (1971). Child's play. New York: John Wiley & Sons, Inc.

Nicholson, S. (October, 1971). How not to cheat children: The theory of loose parts. Landscape Architecture, 30-34.

Noren-Bjorn, E. (1982). The impossible playground (A trilogy of play--Vol. 1: Why?). West Point, NY: Leisure Press.

Page, J. (1976). All you need is love: An investigation of children, their development and the environment in which they play. Unpublished masters thesis, University of Florida.

Roberton, M. A., & Halverson, L. E. (1984). Developing children: Their changing movement. Philadelphia: Lea & Febiger.

Shaw, L. G. (1976). The Playground: The Child's Creative Learning Space (HIMH Report). Gainsville, Florida: College of Architecture, University of Florida.

Thompson, D. (In Press). Swings, Slides and climbing equipment. In L. D. Bruya & S. J. Langendorfer (Eds.), Where our children play: Elementary school Playground Equipment. Washington, DC: AAHPERD, AALR-COP.

U. S. Consumer Product Safety Commission. (March, 1975). Hazard Analysis: Playground Equipment (Bureau of Epidemiology). Washington D.C.: U.S. Government Printing Office.

University Of Iowa, Accident Prevention Section. (October, 1973). Public Playground Equipment: Product Investigation Report (No. FAA 73-6). Iowa City, Iowa: Institute of Agricultural Medicine.

Williams, H.G. (1983). Perceptual and Motor Development. Englewood Cliffs, NJ: Prentice-Hall, Inc.

CHAPTER 3

PLAYGROUND EQUIPMENT: A DESIGNER'S PERSPECTIVE

b y

Jay Beckwith
Play Structure Design Consultant

After many years of designing children's play environments, it has become clear that successful play structures for children meet their developmental needs.   Throughout these years of design and hands-on construction of over 200 community built play structures and four commercial systems, a series of "school-of-hard-knock" understandings have lead to environments which can be described as "developmental."

For many years the only way to acheive innovative environments was to build them from scratch.   In recent years modular commercial systems have become available which allow the creation of environments adapted to nearly any conceivable situation.   The pool of information now available about children's development and the play structures which support that development is now sufficiently well understood so that a fairly straight forward but detailed process can now be followed.

Design Considerations for Contemporary Play Structures

The design of play structures, which have established worth, are based on several succinct statements or rules (Beckwith, 1983b). These rules can be grouped into the following categories: 1) safety, 2) developmental needs of children and 3) structural requirements of equipment and its environment.

Considerations: Safety

• **Challenge or Hazard.** When discussing safety it is best to make a distinction between "challenge" and "hazard." The goal of playground safety programs is NOT to remove excitement and challenge but rather to control hazard. Clearly children seek out and enjoy the stimulation of challenge (Beckwith, 1985a; Ellis, 1973). The literature on play behavior supports the notion that access to such challenges is fundamental to human development (Herron & Sutton-Smith, 1971; Redl, 1959).

The fundamental difference between a challenge and a hazard is that a hazard is something which is hidden, or at least not perceived by the child. A challenge, on the other hand, is something the child may see as dangerous. The design challenge is to create an environment which appears "dangerous" but has been designed to reduce the occurence of injury (see Figure 3.1). Thus, both a sound design and a realistic playground safety program must be grounded in an awareness of the children's powers of perception and comprehension as they develop over time.

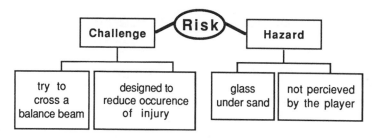

Figure 3.1   The difference between challenge and hazard is important to the overall concept of safety on the playground.

• **Fall Absorbing Materials Under Play Equipment** [1]

The United States Consumer Product Safety Commission (USCPSC) reports that falls are the number one cause of injury in children who play on playground equipment (USCPSC, 1975; NRPA, 1976; USCPSC, 1980). As a result of the danger to players from falls which occur as a natural part of play (Hewes, 1974; Beckwith, 1979, 1983a, 1985b; Bruya,1985) and at the prompting of several designers in the field, the USCPSC adopted a general call for safety surfaces under playgrounds, similiar to the much earlier call of professionals in 1931 National Recreation Association, 1931). As a result of this concern, several suggested standards for surfaces under equipment were developed; eg. all materials judged to be safe must reduce the force of any fall to under 200g.

Unfortunately, this suggestion has not been closely adhered to despite the current trend by manufacturers to place strong warnings on their catalogues indicating that fall absorbing safety surfaces must be used under equipment (Landscape Structures Inc, 1985; Hags, 1985; Iron Mountain Forge, 1987 [2]; Miracle, 1987). As a result of the continued need for surfaces to protect children from falls, and an increase in use of new linked structure formats for playgrounds, it is now more important than ever to install surfaces which absorb force under equipment. The following addresses this issue.

1. Wood Derived Cushions

The principal wood product used for surfacing under play equipment is bark nuggets of from 1/2 inch to 1 inch screen size. The fall absorbing characteristic of this material is due primarily to its compressibility.

Table 3.1   Listed below are the characteristics of wood derived materials used as a fall absorbing safety surface under play equipment.

Wood Derived Materials — Characteristics
Advantages
• Good force absorption when installed to an 8" or more depth • Non-abrasive to flooring surfaces when children track it into the school building after play
Disadvantages
• Will retain water • Will decompose over time • Abrades over time and use • Players may have allergic reactions to its dust • Wooden equipment will deteriorate more quickly when placed within this surface • Cost may be high* • Maintenance expense for replacement may be frequent and costly • Materials will overflow retainer wall

* Sawdust maybe used as an inexpensive sustitute but it retains water and decomposes even more quickly than do bark nuggets.

However, bark nuggets tend to retain water and decompose over time. Their softness allows them to abrade which accelerates this process. Thus, after a relatively short period the nuggets are reduced to a soil like compost with the compressibility factor severely reduced. The gradual degrading of compressibility can make bark nuggets an unsatisfactory surfacing material rather quickly following installation. The real danger when this material is chosen for use under a play structure is that the top surface may disguise the compaction which lies below.

Other negatives associated with wood derived materials include: 1) some children are allegic to bark dust, 2) equipment installed in such material will tend to suffer rapid deterioration, especially in those parts which are wooden e.g. posts, 3) initial cost of installation can be high (especially in some parts of our nation which do not have lumbermills), 4) maintenance attention on a frequent basis is necessary since wood derived cushions spread rather easily outside of the retainer wall, and 5) maintenance attention is required on a regular basis since wood derived surfaces must be replaced due to decomposition and reduction to compost (see Table 3.1). In addition to absorbing the force of falls, the benifit of a wood derived fall cushion is that it is not very abrasive when tracked into buildings.

2. Inorganic Cushions

Inorganic materials such as sand and pea-gravel are the materials most frequently chosen for fall absorbing surfaces under play equipment. But as with wood derived cushions, inorganic materials also possess characteristics which recommend them and characteristics which lessen their effectiveness.

Since it has no compressibility, the fall absorbing characteristic of inorganic materials is due solely to its ability to assume the form of the falling object. This serves to spread the area of impact while increasing its duration. An impact that takes longer to occur over a larger area of the body is less injurious than a quick impact in which the force of the fall is focused in a small area.

To achieve this result the inorganic particles must be round in shape and as uniform in size as possible. However, particles 1/32 of an inch or less will be significantly affected by the surface tension of water and tend to bind together when wet, thus reducing its ability to absorb force. Particles larger than 1/4th of an inch have sufficient mass and may potentially cause serious eye injury when thrown (see Figure 3.2).

Loose Fall Absorbing Safety Surface Recomended Sizes

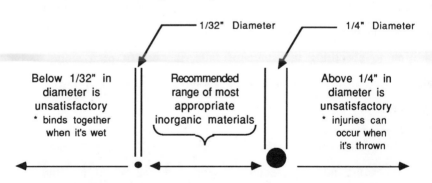

Figure 3.2 The size of the round particles of inorganic material is important to consider when selecting a fall absorbing safety surface under the play equipment.

Inorganic materials of the type required are produced by interaction with water and they exist in river and ocean deposits in many areas. These materials have several names some of which are listed here: 1) washed river bed sand, 2) grain, 3) bird's eye, or 4) river washed pea gravel.

Other considerations associated with inorganic surfaces are also important (see Table 3.2). The species of stone of which these products are made effects the longevity of the installation. Inorganic materials which are derived from hard rock will last longer than those composed of soft stone particles. Since inorganic materials are composed of small rocks, the weight of inorganic materials is quite high making transportation its major expense. Maintenance may also become a problem since inorganic materials spread easily outside the retainer wall simply as a result of the play of children.

Table 3.2 The characteristics of inorganic materials are important when selecting a safety surface used under a play structure.

Inorganic Materials — Characteristics

Advantages

- Excellent fall absorption at 8" depth
- Is readily available with round shape, and uniform size characteristics
- Inexpensive material
- Long lasting when harder inorganic materials are purchased

Disadvantages

- Abrasive to floor surfaces when players track it into the school
- Narrow range of allowable sizes
  1) too small - will bind together
  2) too large - will cause injury when thrown
- Must be river washed (round shaped) to function properly
- Must be generated from hard species of stone
- Major expense can be incurred if it is transported a long way
- Material will overflow the retainer wall

3. Rubber Surfaces

Rubber has been used on playgrounds for decades. The traditional form is a 1-inch thick interlocking mat with a waffle pattern on the underside. When tested by the U.S. Consumer Product Safety Commission (1975), traditional rubber matting surface performed satisfactorily for falls less than 4 feet in height.

In the last 10 years another rubber surfacing material has been used with increasing frequency (Reese, 1985). Chopped tire, when installed to a 6-inch depth, significantly out performs all other available fall absorbing materials. Like inorganic and wood derived cushions, chopped tire will spread ouside its retainer wall to some extent. However, nothing can be done to inorganic or wood derived materials to prevent them from dispersing.

To prevent dispersing in rubber base materials some suppliers mix chopped rubber with a flexible plastic binder. When a small amount of binder is added the material retains most of its fall attenuating characteristics and thus remains effective as a fall absorbing safety surface. But, the plastic bond surface tends to deteriorate with wear and is subject to vandalism. To counteract this fact a skin is added. This skin usually consists of either binder material or artificial turf (see Figure 3.3).

Rubber Safety Surface

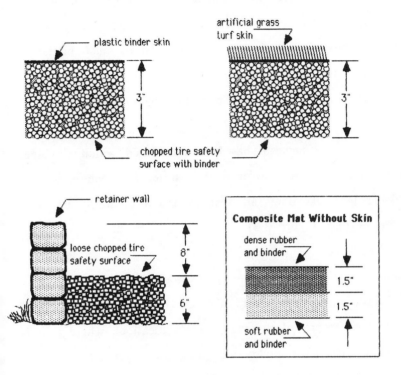

Figure 3.3   Chopped tires can be used as a safety surface either as a loose material or in combination with a plastic binder used to form the material into a mat.

Such composite materials are available up to 3-inches thick for protection in the event of a 10 foot fall. However, some suppliers increase the durability of their composite rubber material by adding more binder. Unfortunately the amount of binder required to stabilize the mixture not only increases the cost significantly but also reduces the composite's fall absorbing ability. If to much binder is added without consideration for the resultant loss in resiliency this bound material can fall below the minimum requirements as a safety surface.

Recently a new material has been introduced which combines dense rubber particles and binder over a softer less dense sub-base. This produces both excellent fall absorption and durability but at premium prices (see Figure 3.3).

4. Drainage

Drainage is the most frequently overlooked aspect of playground installation. In most sites few investments have better cost/benefits than improved drainage. Even locations where rain is not a problem often have muddy play areas due to irrigation. Positive drainage utilizing french drains or equivalent systems under structures are recommended for most installations.

The selection of a site for equipment installation is extremely important. The site must be essentially level if loose organic, inorganic or rubber materials are to remain in place. Special consideration must be given to locations under swings and at the end of slides, because they tend to become the lowest points of the playground and need the most active drainage system.

5. Edge Details

The category signified by the label "Edge Details" includes examination and consideration of: 1) use and fall zones, 2) retainer walls and 3) surrounding maintenance zones. Each of these categories is important when considering the treatment of the safety surface and the details which surround its use and its maintenance.

a) Use and Fall Zones. Planning edge details for play structure boundries require consideration of two important concepts if borders are to be established at appropriate distances from the equipment. These concepts include *use zones* and *fall zones*.

A *use zone* is made up of spaces which surround the equipment and through which the players are likely to pass during use of a specific piece of equipment. For example, the traditional slide has a use zone that extends approximately 6 feet past the end of the exit chute (Carter, Bruya, & Fowler, 1983) to provide space for decceleration following slide exit. In addition, approximately 6 feet to each side of the slide structure is considered a use zone since this is the space through which children return to repeat the use of the slide. The use zone at the entrance end of the traditional slide is between 6 and 10 feet long accounting for the use line that often accompanies the traditional slide on a high use playground (see Figure 3.4).

The *use zone* consideration dictates to the designer how closely grouped traditional equipment can be placed while still serving adequately the function for which it was designed. Use zones are frequently determined after observing children use prototypes of new equipment.

The *fall zone* includes a determination of the space needed around a piece of equipment in which safe falls can occur (see Figure 3.4). For traditional equipment the fall zone is about the equivalent of the use zone or approximately 6 feet all around the structure. To provide additional safety, fall zones also should be calculated another way with the greatest zone measurement used as the size of the fall zone. For every foot of equipment elevation add one foot of fall zone. Thus, for all equipments under 6 feet the normal 6 foot fall zone is adequate. However, for a seven foot structure the fall zone demension increases to 7 feet. An eight foot structure would require a minimum fall zone demension of 8 feet.

The fall zone concept is applied differently for traditional and for contemporary or linked formatted play structures. Particular attention should be given in the case of traditionally formatted equipment to keeping the fall zones free of other equipment since falls to other pieces of equipment is reported by the USCPSC (1980) as being a substantial source of injury. When falls to other pieces of traditional equipment are considered, it takes little time to understand just how lethal a fall of any distance from one bar to another bar can be.

Traditional Playground Equipment

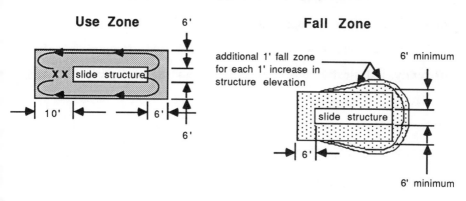

Figure 3.4 The use zone and the fall zone frequently overlap.

Some years ago, Bowers (1977) recognized the safety value of using a pyramid design for play structures. The use of pyramiding removes many precipitous falls inherent on vertical structures. One example of applying the pyramiding concept is to embed a long slide in a hillside. More recently Bruya (1979; 1985) has utilized this concept in the development of a net system on post and deck structures to achieve an "intermediate safety system".

Large linked format play structures approach the pyramiding concept when they are designed with adjacent decks with differentials of 16" or less (see Figure 3.5). Unfortunately some commercial systems rely on internal ladders and have deck height differentials of 36" and even 48". This is designed in this way since it is more economical but it introduces a hazard these systems were developed to eliminate.

However, on the linked structure, the falls are more likely to occur for a short distance (12"-18") and from an event to a deck.

Since decks or platforms are rather wide and flat surfaced, it is usually much easier to regain one's balance following a fall. Thus, the fall zone concept when applied to the linked structure is defined differently. Basically, this means that although the concept for, and the size of the space of the fall zone is approximately the same as that dicussed for traditional equipment, the materials found within the spaces may be different (i.e. platforms or incline ramps).

Playground Equipment Arranged in Linked Format

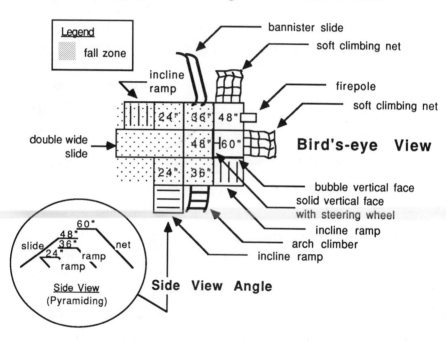

Figure 3.5 The concept of fall zone is slightly modified for application to linked structures which employ the pyramiding concept.

b) **Retainer Walls.** The placement of, or minimum set back from the equipment to the border or retaining wall around the playground is recommended to be 6 feet; plus 2 feet for each 1 foot f equipment height above 4 feet. Certain equipment, such as wings, require larger use and fall zones. Unfortunately , there have een no studies undertaken which determine the exact demensions f the use or fall zones for traditional or contemporary pieces of quipment laid out in either a separated or linked format. onsidering the impact that this type of study could have on the mount of space required for a play structure and additional fall ushion costs which extremely conservative specifications could npose, it would seem advisable from an economic frame of eference, that investigations be designed and undertaken to answer his question.

In spite of the lack of research data, if it is assumed that the lacement of the retainer according to the dimensions mentioned, it not to difficult to understand the visual impact of the retaining all used to contain loose materials. Care taken with the installation f the retainer wall will not only enhance the appearance of the nvironment but can have a significant impact on maintenance equirements.

Wood used for retainer walls must be treated for ground ontact to prevent rotting. However, many of the chemicals used to eat wood are toxic. To prevent contact with children, it is advisable install a non-treated wooden cap over the treated lumber. When oncrete is selected as the building material for the retainer wall, ooden caps are also recommended to reduce the harshness of the dge during contact and to reduce the likelyhood of broken glass eing thrust into the environment as children throw bottles to watch em explode on the edge of the concrete. Recently rubber curbs

63

edge of the concrete. Recently rubber curbs have been introduced and offer an appealing, although costly, alternative.

When loose materials are used, retainer walls can even be constructed of berms covered with grass. This is an effective solution provided that care is taken with details so that mowing can be accomplished with standard practices. It is also extremely important, especially in the case of grass covered berms, that irrigation and proper drainage can occur.

The height of the retainer used to contain loose safety surface materials is determined by two factors: 1) the ability to retain loose material and 2) the creation of a potential trip hazard. Logically, the higher the barrier, the better the retention of loose material. In practice, 8 inches above the fall absorbing material appears to contain all but intentionally thrown material while providing the smallest possible trip hazard.

Retainer Wall Construction Techniques

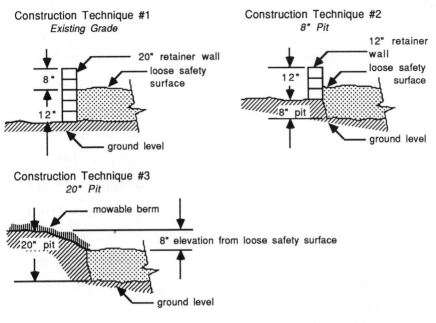

Construction Technique #1
Existing Grade

20" retainer wall
loose safety surface
8"
12"
ground level

Construction Technique #2
8" Pit

12" retainer wall
loose safety surface
12"
8" pit
ground level

Construction Technique #3
20" Pit

mowable berm
20" pit
8" elevation from loose safety surface
ground level

Figure 3.6 Three variations or techniques can be used for containing loose safety surface material. Two of these include the construction of a retainer wall.

The trip hazard caused by the retainer wall exists going both in and out of the play area. Several different techniques have been developed in the attempt to deal the trip hazard caused by the construction of a retainer for loose safety surface.

The first technique includes building a retaining wall on top of the existing grade (see Figure 3.6). If 12 inches of ground cover is added within the confines of the retainer wall but over existing grade, which greatly simplifies drainage requirements, then the approach height from outside the retainer wall would be 20 inches; 12 inches of wall used around loose material, and 8 inches of wall

65

above the material used for its containment. Such a detail presents little trip hazard when approaching the environment since it must be intentionally climbed. A minor hazard exists on exit however, since the child may be unaware of the additional 8 inch climb over and 20 inch drop to ground level when exiting the play environment.

The second technique employs an 8 inch pit with an additional 12 inch barrier; 4 inches of the barrier are used for holding loose material to grade and 8 inches are used for containing or keeping the loose material in the pit. Although this technique reduces the climb over upon entrance, the same trip hazard is presented upon exit as with the previous technique, but with a smaller 12 inch drop to ground level (see Figure 3.6). The problem of drainage of the play environment following a storm or heavy irragation is increased with technique #2.

One additional technique has been developed and used extensively in the Ysleta Independent School District (YISD) located in the El Paso, Texas area. This technique includes digging a 20" pit and backfilling with loose material. Although there is nothing to climb upon entry into the environment, the step off of the 8" edge into a pit can surprise some players, and result in a stumble. But clearly, falling into a sand, pea gravel or rubber base loose safety surface is of less concern than exit falls of equal or greater distance onto hard surfaces. This is especially true when the use and fall zone dimensions outlined earlier are adhered to, thus providing the space necessary to stumble and recover prior to potential collision with equipment (see Figure 3.6).

Problems which can occur when employing this technique usually are concerned with drainage. If this technique is selected for use, it is advisable to position the pit, and the structure within the pit, on a small knoll, thus circumventing the need for long drainage trenches (see Figure 3.7). The Ysleta solution was even more simple than this. Since they receive so little rain each year and do not irrigate, presents no problem at all.

Structure Placement on a Knoll

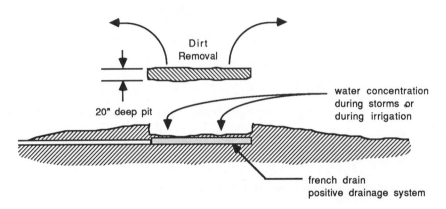

Figure 3.7   When using a pit positioned on top of a knoll to contain loose safety surface material, a french drain is a good example of a positive drainage system.

When any of the retainer wall techniques suggested are surrounded by grass, they are acceptable alternatives. However, when a retainer wall built using any one of these techniques is surrounded by concrete, the trip hazard upon exit is increased. The assumption is that children are distracted upon leaving the environment, trips may occur on the edge of the pit and onto the concrete. Usually this problem is not major in scope since the slower locomotion pattern required in a thick loose safety surface material

67

decreases the rate of exit and thus, the severity of potential injury from a trip.

However, it is essential that additional research be conducted concerning the trip hazard caused by retainer walls. Only through information gained from controlled studies will necessary questions concerning safe play be answered.

c) **Surrounding Maintenance Zone.** The maintenance zone surrounds the surface material retainer wall and extends out about 5 feet from it. This zone is the area where significant future maintenance may be required if designers do not carefully consider the loose material overflow and the need for easy access to the area for quick and efficient servicing. Loose safety surface material which is thrown or kicked over the retainer wall will be deposited in this zone. For example, large amounts of pea gravel which over flows from the retainer wall area onto the grass in the maintenance zone can become a gardener's nightmare during mowing.

A popular solution which has proven to reduce maintenance is the use of a 5 foot surrounding maintenance zone which consists of decomposd compacted granite (see Figure 3.8). This type of zone surfacing allows the accumulation of loose safety material with the least number of problems.

Other materials can be used to surface this zone but often with trade-offs to the safety of those who use the environment. For example, when concrete is used for the surface of the surrounding maintenance zone, ejected, loose safety material acts like roller bearings and can create a significant fall hazard.

68

While a maintenance zone which surrounds the structure retainer wall may not increase the play value of the environment, it can improve the acceptance by maintenance and administrative personnel toward the concept of loose safety surface under playground equipment. This can be an important advantage since elementary school playgrounds of our nation now have a nearly crisis proportion problem in rectifying the fall areas under play equipment.

Surrounding Maintenance Zone

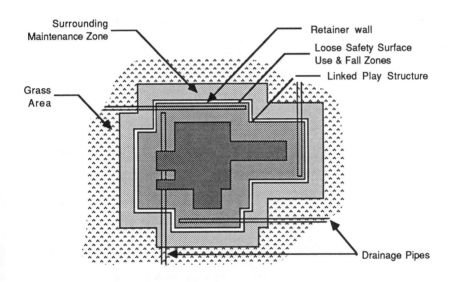

Figure 3.8   The surrounding maintenance zone is the area where the heaviest overflow of loose safety material will accumulate. Using decomposed, compacted granite helps keep the maintenance of this zone less labor intensive.

Consideration: Needs of the Player

• **Human Factors.** Human factors analysis has grown into a science referred to as ergonomics. It would seem that the science of

Ergonomics should also be applied to the development of the play structure. What is known about the physical size and capabilities of children can be applied to the design of play equipment which meets the players' needs (Beckwith, 1982). Yet, it has only been in the last five years that this has been accomplished in even a rudimentary fashion. For decades children have tried to play on equipment composed of wooden sections many times as massive as their bodies, or on slides whose height and size are proportional to children as a multi-story buildings are to adults. The application of ergonomic principles in the case of play structure design would seem to be the simpliest way to rectify many of the problems associated with inappropriate equipment.

Unfortunately, as is the case with some other applications of science, the use of ergonomics in playground design can also lead to inflexible standards: e.g. Standard #1 — If a 6 year old child's step capacity is 12 inches, then ALL steps MUST be 12 inches. Standards of this nature would limit the possibilities for design and ignore two of the prime functions of a playground: to challenge and entertain players through the presentation of the unexpected. Thus, from a motivational point of view, it may be better to have steps which vary, and therefore offer challenge, than to establish a scientifically verifiable but inflexible standard. The issue is to know and understand children's capabilities, not to impose them.

• **Social Interaction.** Much traditional play equipment is designed strictly to provide a child with thrills (e.g., the higher the slide or swing the better). Historically, little thought has been given to the obvious fact that children play in small groups (Wade & Ellis,

1971; Scholtz & Ellis, 1975; Ellis & Scholtz, 1978). Thus, for the past 100 years the standard slide has been made for one-child-at-a-time or singular use. Yet, real world children at play 1) go down the slide in groups, 2) run up the slide chute, and 3) play King-of-the-Mountain on the tiny step at the top. All of these behaviors are hazardous and as such were *not intended by design* but are used by children.

A more appropriate design process for play equipment would take into account the actual behaviors of children and would make every effort to accommodate these normal and predictable play patterns (for example, it is quite straight forward to widen the slide, reduce the over-all height of the slide structure and place a platform at the top to reduce fall risks and increase social interaction). Designers must learn to create equipment for group use. This is not simply providing room in which a group can play, but to ask the question, "What behaviors can be expected from a group of children playing on a piece of equipment?" To answer this question, designers may use the writings of experts in the field (Thompson, 1976), or may design from day-to-day observation and their experience with children, in order to add features that will interest and support the interactions of several children at once.

Consideration: Structural Characteristics

• **Linked or Unified Format.** Traditional thinking, based on play equipment as miniature amusement rides, maintains that each event needs to be separated to avoid 'crowding.' Unfortunately this produces "queuing-up" for turns which can result in injuries as children engage in horse play. The modern or contemporary, linked playground creates traffic flow corridors using platforms which provide open spaces within the structure. Spaces on these platforms also act as stages for observation or dramatic play.

Another vital function that platforms fill is that of an attachment surface for a whole series of optional play events. Research conducted at the University of Florida (Shaw, 1976), and North Texas State University (Bruya, 1985) clearly established the validity of the linked or unified playground concept. In these studies it was demonstrated that when the equipment was linked together or unified, extended periods of play occurred on the structure. When the same equipment was separated, the play pattern became increasingly random and unrelated to the equipment.

•**Play Events - Play Value.** Play value is a term used to described the ability of an environment or device to stimulate and sustain human play behaviors. A key ingredient involved in determining play value is novelty. This leads the child naturally to explore. Thus, begins the process by which children learn by experiment and thereby determine their relationship to the environment in which they live (see Figure 3.9).

The Play Process

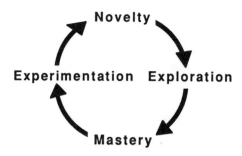

Figure 3.9 The play process signals a chain of events which eventually leads the player to experimentation.

Also, equipment with high play value contains an almost tool-like quality. An excellent example of this characteristic is called Lego Blocks. These seemingly simple blocks are able to support incredibly complex and durable play episodes.

Lego blocks, wet sand, dolls, and balls are all fundamental toys with very high play value. This value grows out of the object's ability to provide an appropriate vehicle for the child's self expression (intrinsically motivated activity) and the rich options for experimentation which they generate. Thus, when considering playgrounds, it is easiest to think of play events as if they were fundamental toys and the focus of activity rather than as if they are an end in themselves.

However, play events may have high or low play value partially depending upon the developmental levels of the children. Designing equipment to more closely match children's actual play patterns increases the play value of the equipment. For example, a wide slide has more play value than a narrow slide because it offers

73

many more behavioral options: options which lead to exploration and finally to expermentation. This is borne out in studies which examine the play patterns used and the duration of play on selected items within a playground (Campbell, Bruya & Fowler, 1983; Bruya, Robbins & Fowler, 1983 a&b).

• **Events Per Child.** Years of personal interviews conducted with regular classroom teachers who act as playground monitors have indicated that they clearly understand the greatest source of playground behavior problems; competition for limited play resources. Lines of children waiting their turn are the most easily recognized symptom of the problem; this leads to "cuts" and horseplay which all too frequently ends up in fighting and/or injury.

To reduce these problems, the planner must begin the process of design by assessing the needs of the school population for which the structure is intended. The next step is to develop a concise inventory of the play activities to be offered based on specific learning objectives. Finally, the planner must determine the number of children to be served by the environment in each of its several use modes; 1) physical education instruction, 2) free play use at recess, and 3) holding area after lunch and before and after school.

As an example, in general, children fourth grade or above have little real need for play equipment (Longino & Bruya, 1983). Conversely, first grade children spend a majority of their time involved in and around the play apparatus. These two age groups can be used as upper and lower age limits for play structure use. A general "rule of thumb" used to determine the equipment requirements for an elementary school is one-third the total population of grades one through three. Thus, a school of 300 first through third grade children would need enough play equipment to serve the needs of 100 players.

To determine how much equipment is needed to serve 100 children, it is necessary to calculate the "carrying capacity" of each event. The carrying capacity for one play event is equal to the number of children who can occupy the equipment safely. These capacities for each event are combined to arrive at the total number of children the environment will adequately serve.

On large interconnected play structures, hours of observation have lead to the conclusion that the linked format environments have a "carrying capacity" of approximately twice that of traditional separate play event arrangements. After realizing that additional numbers of players were being carried by the structure it became obvious that something was occurring on the interconnected linked structure that did not occur on traditionally formatted equipment. Thus, the importance of the "observer phenomena" during play was considered.

More careful observation led to the conclusion that only about half of the children carried by the structure engaged in what was considered to be active play. At first, it appeared that inactive children were waiting their turn. This conclusion was rejected following repeated cycling of active players through events with inactive players standing by.

An alternative conclusion appears closer to the truth. The inactive children carried by the structure during active play by others, must be learning vicariously as a form of readiness for activity. Thus, the platforms or decks characteristic of the linked format structures serve a dual function which increases "carrying capacity." First they serve as a staging area for active players who are engaged with the environment while occupied during play. Second, platforms and/or decks serve as observation posts where children collect information and prepare mentally (i.e. learn) to participate in a more active and perhaps more complex and challenging play pattern.

Another example will indicate how the "carrying capacity" concept can be used to assist planners in the design of the environment. Clearly, a standard belt seat swing is suitable for only one child. A traditional slide can be simultaneously used by three or four children depending upon its height and width. As an example of using the carrying capacity of these two pieces of equipment to estimate the needs of our example school of 100 children, 50 swing seats and 15 slides would be required to adequately meet the needs of the players when the structures themselves are organized in a traditional non-linked format.

However, when these same events are connected to a linked, interconnected or unified structure format the number of children the structure will carry increases dramatically. Although designers do not yet completely understand the mechanism by which this increase occurs, and the previous discussion only provides some initial indications which need further study, general consensus among designers has lead to the conclusion that the platforms used in a linked or unified structure interact with the event to substantially increase its carrying capacity. Thus, to complete our example, a typically interconnected structure of ten decks and 20 events (most of which are specially designed for small group use) can be used to accomodate the play patterns of 100 children (Beckwith, 1979b).

• **Semi-Enclosed Spaces.** The need and value of semi-enclosed spaces has been well understood by early childhood and child development specialists for years. Play houses and small reading cubicles are two examples of such spaces often added by teachers to their environments. From a learning perspective, semi-enclosed spaces seem to be desirable. However, it is noteworthy that the typical school playground, consisting of pipe frame equipment, provides none of these spaces.

The rationalization used for this oversight is that such spaces present supervision difficulties. This is only true however, of fully enclosed spaces. Children do not need, nor self-select fully enclosed environments. What is required is a partial barrier which provides a *sense* of enclosure. Such protection is needed for the development of small group interaction and the consequent maturation of a sense of self.

Translucent materials or limited visual blocks of two square feet or less are useful for creating semi-enclosed spaces. In this way playground supervisors can maintain an awareness of the locality and activity of the players while at the same time the children enjoy the sense of enclosure.

The provision of such designs is certainly possible and could go a long way toward putting the "play" back into playgrounds. Design solutions *are* possible and manufacturers *will* produce them, if schools begin to signal their willingness to purchase equipment which features semi-enclosed spaces. To initiate the development of more appropriate environments for children which include semi-enclosed spaces, a large school district or state-wide educational organization would need to issue purchasing guidelines which specified such features.

• **Modularity.** The concept of modularity, first introduced with commercial wood pole systems, has proven valuable for a variety of reasons. A well designed modular system allows the creation of very complex environments from a small vocabulary of simple parts. The resulting structures with interchangeable parts are easy to maintain, and easy to change. Older and more traditional systems prevented field modification to adapt them to local conditions or adjust to changing demands. Modular systems are a better investment since they can be easily maintained and adapted after installation.

Design Checklist

To improve the quality of play structures available for young children, both the structure itself and its ongoing maintenance are important considerations. The following checklist is intended to provide a guide for decision making concerning the design and operation of a high quality play environment.

Design Checklist for Schoolyard Playgrounds

Safety Surfacing

Loose Material - organic and inorganic

☐ A minimum of eight inches of safety surface must be available under all structures.

☐ Impact zones under swings and the slide exit chute should be 24 inches in depth.

☐ Inorganic materials selected for use must be round.

☐ Inorganic materials selected for use must be between the sizes of 1/32" and 1/4" in diameter.

Rubber Material

☐ Specifications for fall absorbing qualities of rubber mat must meet the CPSC required 200g impact attenuation guideline for the height of the specific play structure.

    e.g. 1 inch mat - 48 inches in height (total height-not deck)

         2 inch mat - 64 inches in height

         3 inch mat - 120 inches in height

☐ Chopped tire safety surface must be 4" or greater in depth.

Drainage

☐ Provision must be made for quick removal of water - French drains are one system which should be considered.

Layout

☐ Fall zones which surround traditional equipment must be free of obstacles.

☐ Player traffic routes in the use zones must be large enough to provide multi-directional movement.

☐ Natural sight lines must remain open so that the play ground may be monitored.

Entrapment

☐ Five to seven inch openings must be removed or filled to prevent head entrapment.

☐ "V" shaped intersections between parts of the equipment, which are 1) 55o or less, 2) 10o above horizontal and, 3) more than 24" above the ground must be removed or filled to prevent entrapment.

☐ All parts of the playground including connecting hardware and hand holds must not be capable of entangling clothing. This includes pipe extensions used for hold holds.

Corners, Edges and Protrusions

☐ The edges and corners of all objects in the enviroment must be radiused (rounded).

☐ All sharp edges within the environment must be eliminated.

☐ All pipe ends must be capped.

☐ All protrusions from connecting hardware must have a permanently affixed protective covering.

☐ All protrusions, even if covered, must not exten greater than the diameter of the object.

Specific Pieces of Equipment

Slides

☐ High density polyethylene slides are preferred over stainless steel slides.

☐ Stainless steel slides must face north away from the angle of direct sunlight.

☐ Fiberglass slides are not a good choice since they are easy to vandalize and they splinter under severe stress.

☐ Slide chute run-out or deceleration area must be within 0o to 4o of horizontal and at least 16 inches long.

☐ Total slide incline must not exceed 30o.

☐ Slide height must not exceed 80" in elevation from the ground. Slides mounted in the side of hillsides may be of any length as long as the total fall distance from the slide surface to the ground does not exceed 80" at any point.

☐ Slides designed with a wheel chair dismount area are preferred.

☐ Slides designed with an access ramp parallel to the slide chute are preferred.

Swings — Standard

☐ 'S' hooks must be closed

☐ The distance between seats and stationary supports or other seats must be at least 18 inches.

☐ Seats must be slash proof.

☐ Suspended masses, such as animals, must not be used unless documentation is provided which establishes that they pass the USCPSC 200g impact test.

☐ Swings with seats designed for proper positioning and support are preferred.

Swings — Tire

☐ Support beams must be two times the swing height plus 48 inches.

☐ Ball joint bearings must have at least 170 degrees of swing.

☐ Universal joint bearings must be covered with a durable, flexible shield.

Climbers

☐ Climbers should be of the "fall free" design, i.e., arches and domes, which do not present obstacles on which to fall as do the 'cube' and most theme type of climbers.

☐ Climbers are the most frequent source of entrapment and must be carefully examined for this problem.

☐ Link climbers to other structures to generate additional activity and reduce 'king-of-the-mountain' games.

☐ Flexible climbers (i.e. rope and chain net) offer the highest motor challenge and greatest popularity with children.

Balance Equipment

☐ Balance activities have been identified as having significant value.

☐ Soft balance activities (i.e. rope and chain nets) have the greatest value and appeal.

☐ Suspended balance activities place large stress forces on play structures. Check to insure that designs are able to accommodate such loads.

☐ Suspended balance activity equipment must be frequently inspected for wear at the connection points.

☐ Stability and traction surfaces on balance events must be included as a part of the design.

Upper Body Development Equipment

☐ Check to insure that play structure linkage does not provide ready access to the top of upper body play events.

☐ To develop skill and upper shoulder girdle fitness each playground should have several upper body play events at various levels of challenge. Listed by degrees of least to most difficult, upper body development equipment include: turning bars, chinning bars, parallel bars, horizontal ladders, track rides, and ring treks.

☐ Linking and/or grouping upper body events improves their utilization.

Equipment to Support Locomotor Development

☐ Walking   ☐ Running   ☐ Jumping
☐ Hopping   ☐ Gallopping
☐ Skipping   ☐ Sliding   ☐ Leaping

Equipment to Support Non-Locomotor Development

☐ Pushing   ☐ Pulling   ☐ Swinging
☐ Swaying   ☐ Lifting   ☐ Carrying
☐ Bending   ☐ Stretching

Equipment to Support Manipulative Actions

☐ Kicking   ☐ Striking   ☐ Catching
☐ Throwing

Equipment Which Supports the Following Uses

☐ Level changes in the body
☐ Level changes in distance off the ground

☐ Options for and uses of six directions: up, down, forward, backward, left, and right

☐ Otions and choices are provided for the selection of at least two pathways to each event

Spinners or Merry-Go-Rounds

☐ In general spinners are not recommended for school settings unless they are 4 feet or less in diameter and are equiped with speed governors.

☐ Spinners must have rails which fully enclose the platform.

☐ The distance from the bottom edge of the platform and the fall surface should not exceed 6 inches.

☐ All protrusions or projections must be eliminated from any spinning equipment.

☐ The 'running track' zone around spinners which players use to push the spinner tends to become worn and thus becomes a low spot on the playground. This zone should have double deep surfacing material and positive drainage.

☐ Designs which provide access to and support for disabled users are preferred.

Purchase and Installation Considerations

Undertaking the creation or renovation of a quality play environment is an expensive and time consuming project. Although the development of an educationally sound playground may appear to be straight forward, a major committment is required to complete such a goal.

In addition to the basic design guidelines and checklists
anners also must consider principles which govern several
ditional factors beyond the equipment itself. Some of these
clude: 1) the nature and the extent of parent and community
volvement, 2) budgeting and fund raising, 3) receiving value from
ur purchases, 4) use instructions, 5) installation quality control, 6)
gn-off procedure, 7) long term maintenance, and 8) its use in the
ysical education curriculum.

ature and Extent of Parent and Community Involvement

After struggling to produce a workable model for building your
vn playground as a community project, the playground movement
ew and matured. Since that time our society and the playground
dustry itself has changed.

The initial motivation to design and build custom playgrounds
rung from frustration with commecial manufacturers which at that
ne offered rocket ships on the one hand and massive wooden
onoliths on the other. Since that time many of the design goals
poused in the Build Your Own Playground. . . manuscript (Hewes,
75) have been adopted by manufacturers, thus making
ntemporary manufactured equipment more attractive and suitable
r use in the schools.

Since the early '70s the liability climate in our nation has
anged considerably as well. While community paticipation in the
velopment of a playground is still an excellent idea, the nature of
at involvement has changed. Now, because of the potential for
wsuits and the extent of the expertise needed to design structures,

it is unwise for parent groups to design and construct their own playground equipment.

Over the years, it has become more evident that parent designed and constructed play structures, which were based on an interpretation of the currently available literature on the issue, provided certain benifits for play which now are overwhelmingly offset by maintenance, liability, and safety problems. To reduce the cost of maintenance and the number and severity of design induced safety problems, it is wise to purchase one of the new modular systems and limit volunteerism to installation according to manufacturers' specifications. In this way the community involvement concept can continue.

Many manufacturers offer services which support such community involvement. These services include the use of factory-trained personnel to oversee installation. Even if a small fee is paid for such a service, the expense is offset by improvement in the overall quality and speed of the construction.

To increase community participation, parents can be involved in the construction and installation of the retainer wall and loose safety surface materials since these must be site built. They also can assist in landscaping tasks related to the development of the playground. Such volunteer efforts can easily save up to as much as 50% of the installation cost of the project.

Many attempts to cut costs are generally detrimental to the overall quality of the environment. For example, to save freight costs, school groups may purchase wood products from the local lumber yard. These typically do not have the necessary non-toxic wood treatment and already include the cost of their transportation hidden in their price. Worse yet is the practice of using recycled materials which are likely to lack durability of todays play equipment. While such cost cutting efforts may save a few dollars initially, they greatly expand the time required for construction, significantly increase liability, and produce maintenance problems for the life of the playground (see Figure 3.10).

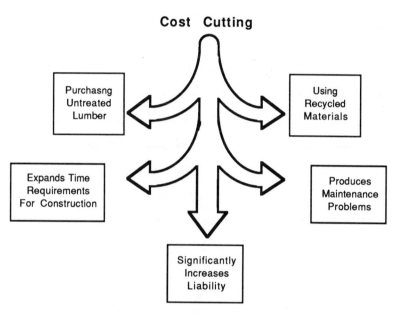

Figure 3.10 Some forms of cost cutting can prove detrimental to the overall quality of the play environment.

Budgeting and Fund Raising

The cost of modern commecial systems ranges from $100 to 150 per child. Thus, the equipment costs for the typical 100 child system would range from $10,000 to $15,000. Generally speaking, the cost differential in equipment is directly related to the size and strength of the system.

Two products which may appear to be quite similar judging by their their catalog pictures in reality may be substantially different. Thus, unless those in charge of purchasing play equipment have considerable experience and/or knowlege and feel confident in their ability to understand detailed specifications, it is an excellent idea to make a field inspection of the products being considered, to be certain of the size, quality, and desired configuration.

Since the initial cost is substantial it is important to consider product durability. By purchasing durable equipment, communities can hedge against the likelihood of additional expense caused by future maintenance requirements. Schools can normally expect a minimum of 10 years service from typical commercial grade equipment. The cost of this play equipment is about $10—$15 per child per year. When purchasing price is viewed in this way, play equipment clearly provides one of the highest cost/benefit ratios of any purchase a school may make.

Receiving Value from the Purchase

The buyer should be aware of 'hidden' costs when purchasing play equipment. One expense which often surprises buyers is freight. Cost increases of from 10 to 15% of the total cost of the environment for freight is not uncommon (see Figure 3.11). In some cases, although not in the case of the public schools sampled in this survey, sales tax will also be added to the total expense.

Professional installation can add still another 25 to 45% to the ırchase (see Figure 3.11). Even if the buyer decides it best to do e installation himself or herself there can be the costs of concrete, e preparation if the site is not level and perhaps the expense of ıle digging.

Generally the second largest capital expense, after the uipment purchase itself, is the expense of the fall absorbing ıterial placed under the structure and within the retainer walls. In ost locations a simple wooden box which contains sand is the most tisfactory and cost effective solution. It is not uncommon for a dwood box with 12" of quality sand to add 25% to the overall cost the total playground catalog price quoted for just the equipment ee Figure 3.11). A reasonable expectation of the total cost of an stalled play structure with ground cover is to double the catalog ıst of the play equipment alone (see Figure 3.11).

Prediction Formula
Total Play Structure Expense

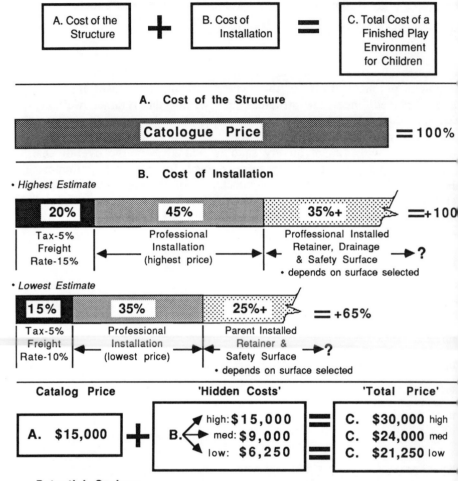

| A. Cost of the Structure | **+** | B. Cost of Installation | **=** | C. Total Cost of a Finished Play Environment for Children |

A. Cost of the Structure

Catologue Price ═ 100%

B. Cost of Installation

• *Highest Estimate*

| **20%** | **45%** | **35%+** | ═ +100 |

| Tax-5% Freight Rate-15% | Professional Installation (highest price) | Proffessional Installed Retainer, Drainage & Safety Surface • depends on surface selected | ➔? |

• *Lowest Estimate*

| **15%** | **35%** | **25%+** | ═ +65% |

| Tax-5% Freight Rate-10% | Professional Installation (lowest price) | Parent Installed Retainer & Safety Surface • depends on surface selected | ➔? |

Catalog Price	'Hidden Costs'	'Total Price'
A. $15,000 **+**	**B.** high: **$15,000** med: **$9,000** low: **$6,250** **=**	C. **$30,000** high C. **$24,000** med C. **$21,250** low

Potential Savings
1. Difference between high and low professional bids = $6,000.
2. Parent installation Retainer wall plus safety surface =10% or $1500.

Figure 3.11   Expense for the turn key construction of a play structure for children usually amounts to about 200% of the listed catalog price of the structure alone.

90

Use Manuals (Manufacturer Suggested)

Perhaps the single most desirable, yet seldom available feature of a playground equipment system is the inclusion of a curriculum manual for use by physical education and classroom teachers. It is logical that such an important and expensive investment be supported by curricular materials for use by the school. In this way the teaching staff in the school could be provided guidance in the instruction of children in safe and educationally beneficial behaviors.

To date only one manufacturer has provided a "use manual" designed for use in the schools (Schoolyard Big Toys, 1979; Schoolyard Big Toys, 1980). While each of these systems have been one of the most broadly accepted features when school districts purchase equipment, they have not been emulated by other manufacturers. The reason for this can be attributed to several factors. Principal among these is that schools do not require a "use manual" as a part of their purchase criteria.

The value of a "use manual" goes well beyond instructional benefits. If schools begin to demand an instructional component when purchasing playground equipment, manufacturers will be forced to improve a selection of play events which provide a wider range of physical, cognitive, and social activities.

An additional benefit, one which is becoming increasingly important, is that such instructional support can take a significant role in the program to manage risk (see Chapter 10). A frequent claim in accident cases is insufficient supervision. Without an established standard of care all such claims must be litigated. While a "use manual" will not eliminate claims, it will provide evidence that an instructonal base exists for use of the playground.

The "use manual" should provide a program of increasing difficulty appropriate for the least developed first grade student through the most advanced third grade student. The goals included in the curriculum should provide latitude for selection, so that students and teachers can work together to determine activities to use on the play structure. Lessons should include motor planning, upper body development, balance and spatial awareness activities, as well as encourage health related fitness (see Chapter 7). In addition provision should be made to include other curriculum areas outside of physical activity (see Chapter 6). A section should also include suggestions and techniques for including children in the governance of their own safe play (see Chapter 4). Finally, within the 'use manual' a system should be outlined by which students can measure and record changes in performance over time.

Installation Quality Control

Even with the best design and highest quality equipment the lack of proper installation can still jeopardize the final quality of the environment. It is of primary importance that the installation be carefully planned and monitered. To accomplish this task a thorough review must be undertaken of: 1) the intallation requirements, 2) manufacturers' sign-off, and 3) long-term maintenance.

• **Installation   Requirements**

The installation of a play equipment has three components. They are: 1) instructions, 2) labor requirements, and 3) assembly.

Instructions.   Modern commercial playground equipment is typically supplied with detailed and thorough installation instructions complete with schematic drawings to guide assembly. At least one company, Kompan of Sweden, which exports equipment throughout the world, has instructions which are totally graphic. This type of installation instruction is the   clearest, the most easily understood, and the overall best type of   installation guide in the industry.

Labor   Requirements.   Typically, the greatest amount of labor involves the excavation of the footing holes.   Some modular systems have posts set at regular intervals and it is a simple matter to lay out the holes and have them pre-dug at the required depth by a fencing company.

Assembly.   Construction using a factory designed and manufactured play structure is a matter of assembling factory made parts.   The modular systems which come with preassembled events and platforms contain the fewest number and type of connectors and are significantly easier to install than are systems which composed of many parts and little in the way of preassembled components.   For the most part, construction requires only the use of hand tools.   Few components are too heavy to be moved by two strong adults.

• **Sign Off Procedure**

Once construction has been completed, a file should be created which documents the purchase and installation of the equipment. The installation instructions should be included in that file.

Historically, once shipped to the buyer, the factory had little continuing involvement. In the current climate of litigation many buyers are requiring a factory representative, generally the regional sales person, inspect the construction upon completion, and send a letter stating that the installation meets factory specifications. This letter is also added to the file. Photographs of the finished structure should be included in the documentation.

Long-Term Maintenance: The Inspection Process

There is considerable variance in the frequency of inspections provided playgrounds across the nation. Not only do similar school districts with similar conditions have quite dissimilar standards for inspection, but the equipment manufacturers also differ greatly in their recommendation for regular inspections.

However, common characteristics of the inspection process have become apparent. Three of the most important appear below.

1. It is a good idea to provide a daily visual review of the play environment, inspecting it for hazards as specified in an approved checklist. Keep a log of these inspections.

2. A "tear down" inspection should be performed periodically, perhaps as often as monthly during heavy use. The purpose of this inspection is to examine features such as bearings and

footings for deterioration as detailed in the manufacturer's specifications and an approved checklist.

3. School districts should develop a comprehensive maintenance program. This must include staff training, provision of inspection checklists, prompt repair of discovered problems, follow-up quality assurance, and detailed documentation (see Figure 3.12).

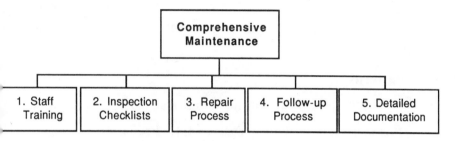

Figure 3.12 A comprehensive maintenance program includes information, material and processes in addition to physical repair.

Inspection Checklists

To insure the quality of our structures available for the play of young children, two inspection processes are important. The first of these is the inspection process which takes place daily, while the second process includes those inspection items which should be the focus of attention at least once a month. In both instances a checklist used to guide decisions concerning inspection of the play environment can help to insure thoroughness. The following checklists for schoolyard playgrounds are provided as models for daily and monthly inspections.

Daily Playground Inspection Checklist

On a daily basis walk through the play area with a general alertness to the condition of the environment. Pay paticular attention to:

Surfacing

☐ Remove foreign objects from the loose safety material surface.

☐ Rake loose surface materials to prevent compaction and to maintain correct depths of surfacing under vital parts of the structure.

Play Patterns

☐ Watch children at play to insure that the equipment is not generating play patterns considered to be unsafe.

Vandalism

☐ Look for signs of vandalism and report them for correction.

Critical Equipment Points

☐ Carefully inspect all moving equipment (e.g. swings and spinners) for damage and wear.

Monthly Playground Maintenance Checklist

Once each month the maintenance crew should carefully spect each play area, paying paticular attention to:

urfacing

☐ Test loose material for 12 inch depth throughout the play environment. Add new material as required.

☐ Inspect the surfacing material for deterioration and compacting.

☐ Inspect the surrounding retainer wall for deterioration.

☐ Verify that drainage systems continue to perform to specification.

tructural Considerations

☐ Move loose surfacing materials and inspect all wooden footings for rot and all metal footings for rust.

☐ Look for exposed, broken or cracked footings.

☐ Inspect and tighten connecting hardware.

☐ Dismantle, inspect, lubricate and reinstall all bearings such as those found on swings and spinners.

☐ Inspect swing seats, chain, and "S" hooks for wear. Be certain "S" hooks are closed.

☐ Check each piece of equipment for stability.

☐ Inspect structural components, especially wood, for deterioration.

☐ Check for sharp edges, splinters and cracks.

☐ Insure that pipe caps and protective coverings are in place.

Vandalism

☐ Inspect for broken and damaged components, with special attention given to safety rails.

☐ Remove graffiti. Re-seal vertical walls when required.

End Notes

1) The information on fall absorbing materials and the checklists which follow specific sections of this document were originally developed for the "Play For All" Conference held in Fall, 1986 at Stanford University, Palo Alto, CA. These original documents have been rewritten for additional clarity and with additional information and are included here with permission.

2) The most complete analysis of safety surfacing material by a manufacturer is that found in the Iron Mountain Forge 1987/88 catalogue.

Bibliography

Beckwith, J. (1979a, January). You can build a playground. American School & University, 28-31.

Beckwith, J. (1979b). Playground planning and fund raising guide for schoolyard BigToys™. Tacoma, WA: Northwest Design Products Inc.

Beckwith, J. (1982, September). It's time for creative play. Parks & Recreation, 37-42.

Beckwith, J. (1983a). Further thoughts on falling. ProData, 1(2), 3.

Beckwith J. (1983b May). Playgrounds for the twenty-first century. Cities & Villages, 21(5), 22-26.

Beckwith, J. (1985a, May/June). Play environments for all children. JOPHERD, 32-35.

Beckwith, J. (1985b). Equipment selection criteria for modern playgrounds. In J.L. Frost and S. Sunderlin (Eds.), When Children Play. Wheaton, MD: Association for Children Education International.

Bowers, L. (August, 1977). Play Learning Centers for Preschool Handicapped Children (U.S.O.E.. Research and Demonstration Project Report). Tampa, Florida: College of Education, University of South Florida.

Bruya, L. D. (1985). Design Characteristics used in playgrounds for children. In J.L. Frost & S. Sunderlin, When children play. Wheaton, MD: Association for Childhood Education International.

Bruya, L.D., Robbins, R. & Fowler, C.L. (June-July, 1983a). Play patterns exhibited by three, four and five year old children when playing on a contemporary tire swing. Presented at the International Conference on Play & Play Environments, Austin, Texas.

Bruya, L.D., Robbins, R. & Fowler, C.L. (June-July,1983b). Preferred use of parts of the play structure by three, four and five year old children. Presented at the International Conference on Play & Play Environments, Austin, Texas.

Bruya, L.D., Carter, C.S. & Fowler, C.L. (June-July, 1983). Position effects as an indicator of play routes on a play structure. Presented at the International Conference on Play & Play Environments, Austin, Texas.

Bruya, L. D., Sullivan, M., & Fowler, C. L. (1979). Safety on the horizontal ladder: An intermediate catch system. In C. Gabbard (Ed.), Texas A&M Conference on Motor Development and Movement Experiences of Children (10-12). College Station, TX: Texas A&M Press.

Campbell, E., Bruya, L.D. & Fowler, C.L. (June-July, 1983). The suspension bridge as a part of a larger play structure and its use rate by children. Presented at the International Conference on Play & Play Environments, Austin, Texas.

Ellis, M.J. (1973). Why people play. Englewood Cliffs, NJ: Prentice-Hall.

Ellis, M.J. & Scholtz, G.J.L. (1978). Activity and play of children. Englewood Cliffs, NJ: Prentice-Hall.

Game Time (1986). Game Time '87: Park and playground equipment. Fort Payne, AL: GameTime, Inc.

Hags (1985). Hags no. 120: Children's play equipment and landscape furniture. Aneby, Sweden: Sweden AB Hags Mekaniska.

Herron, R.E. & Sutton-Smith, B. (1971). Child's play. New York: John Wiley & Sons, Inc.

Hewes, J. (1975). Build your own playground: A source book of play structures, designs, and concepts from the work of Jay Beckwith. Boston: Houghton Mifflin Co.

Iron Mountain Forge (1987). Kid Builders playground equipment. Farmington, MO: Iron Mountain Forge.

Landscape Structures (1985). Landscape Structures/Mexico Forge: Play equipment, sports & fitness, site furnishings catalogue 1986/1987. Delano, Mn: Landscape Structures Inc.

Longino, J.P. & Bruya, L.D. (June-July, 1983). The use of existing play equipment available on a schoolyard playground. Presented at the International Conference on Play & Play Environments, Austin, Texas.

National Recreation Association (1931). Report of committee on standards in playground apparatus (Bulletin No. 2170). New York: The Association.

National Recreation and Park Association (NRPA) (1976). Proposed safety standard for public playground equipment. Arlington, VA: National Recreation and Park Association.

Redl, F. (1959). The impact of game ingredients on children's play behavior. In B. Schaffner (Ed.), Group processes: Transactions of the fourth conference. New York: Josiah Macy, Jr., Foundation, 33-81.

Reese, O. (1985). Cushion Turf-Advertising Flyer. Chicago, IL: Reese Industries, Inc.

Scholtz, G.J.L. & Ellis, M.J. (1975). Repeated exposure to objects and peers in a play setting. Journal of experimental Child Psychology, 19, 445-455.

Schoolyard Big Toys (1979). Use manual: A program of activities for preschool and elementary school children using Schoolyard Big Toys® equipment. Tacoma, WA: Northwest Design Products, Inc.

Schoolyard Big Toys (1980). Hang-Ups™. Tacoma, WA: Northwest Design Products, Inc.

Shaw, L.G. (1976). The playground: The child's creative learning space (MH 20743-04A1). Gainesville, Florida: Bureau of Research, College of Architecture, University of Florida.

Thompson, D. (1976). Space utilization: Criteria for the selection of playground equipment for children. Research Quarterly, 47, 3, 472-483.

United States Consumer Product Safety Commission (April, 1975). Hazard analysis: Playground equipment. Washington DC: U.S. Printing Office.

United States Consumer Product Safety Commission (1980). A handbook for public playground safety (Vol. II : Technical guidelines for equipment and surfacing). Washington DC: U.S. Government Printing Office.

Wade, M.C. & Ellis, M.J. (1971). Measurement of free range activity in children as modified by social and environmental complexity. The American Journal of Clinical Nuitrition, 24, 1457-1460.

PART TWO:

Towards Safe Play On School Playgrounds

CHAPTER 4

DEVELOPING RESPONSIBILITY OF CHILDREN FOR PLAYGROUND SAFETY

by

P. Lowe
Huntsville, Alabama Public Schools

With interest and cooperation among students, faculty, and community, a successful educational program for 'Safe Play' has been developed and implemented on the playground of Farley Elementary School of the Huntsville City Schools, Huntsville, Alabama. The 'Safe Play' program consists of multi-curricular presentations of concepts and activities related to playing without injury. This means that students are challenged to be aware of playing safely in several ways. These include: 1) student council meetings, 2) physical education classes, 3) playground guidelines, 4) poster project, 5) playground safety patrol, 6) the teacher's role, and 7) the objective of the 'Safe Play' program.

Student Council Participation

Farley Elementary School has a very active Student Council which is comprised of an elected student representative from each of the kindergarten through 5th grade classrooms. At the beginning of the school year and at the suggestion of the faculty representative, the Student Council discussed the need for and implementation of a 'Safe Play' program at the school.

The students were very interested in, and enthusiastic about this responsibility. They were asked to take the concept of 'Safe Play' back to their homerooms for discussion with their peers. Their job was to ask the other students for ideas concerning the implementation of a year long safety program on the playground. In this way students of all ages who used the playground and its structures were involved in the initiation of the 'Safe Play' program. Student responsibility for the development, implementation and eventual enforcement of the program was in this way insured. In this instance, a child-oriented 'Safe Play' program was defined as one in which: 1) children designed the original structure of the program with the guidance of the teacher and 2) the program was fine tuned or adjusted by the children as needed changes became obvious (see Figure 4.1). The result of including children in all parts of the initiation and conduct of the program helped create a long term commitment to its ideals and its conduct in the children.

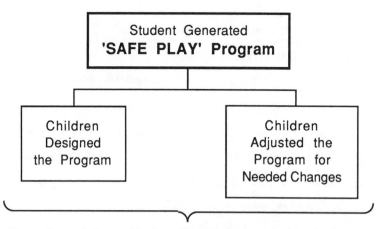

Figure 4.1   The 'Safe Play' program was designed and changed by the
children who used it.

The following suggestions were made at a Student Council meeting, after the representatives had asked their classmates and homeroom teachers to make suggestions for initiating a 'Safe Play' program:

1.   Conduct a Playground Safety Week in September and again in February to maintain the students' awareness that safe play is every student's responsibility.
2.   Ask the students to make posters to display in the school building showing the guidelines for play safety on the playground.
3.   Organize a playground safety patrol: the "classroom helper" of the day (the person who is the messenger, doorholder, line leader, etc.) was designated "playground safety patrol person" for that day.

Physical Education Class Participation

To support the intention of these suggestions, it became obvious that a vehicle was needed for the formation of rules and procedures associated with the playground safety issue. It was decided that the physical education classes would be that vehicle, with part of each class time set aside to complete the guidance of the children's decision making process involving safe play. In this way time was provided to teach children to think through the physical elements of space, balance, force, speed, direction and flow that characterize movement (see Figure 4.2). This was felt to be important since the children would then approach the task of designing a "Safe Play" program with a fairly uniform and consistent vocabulary, and a conceptual understanding which was thought by the faculty to underpin safety on the playground (Kirchner, Cunningham, Warrell, 1978; Brown & Sommer; 1969; Bilbrough & Jones,1968). Through this assigned class time and the discussion of the elements of movement, combined with the active and evolving process of student involvement in decision making, the children seemed to understand, respect, and finally to establish the safety guidelines for each piece of apparatus and for the playground facility as a whole.

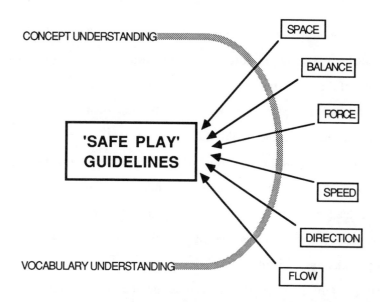

CONCEPT UNDERSTANDING

SPACE

BALANCE

FORCE

'SAFE PLAY' GUIDELINES

SPEED

DIRECTION

VOCABULARY UNDERSTANDING

FLOW

Figure 4.2 The concepts borrowed from movement education were the characteristics of movement used to develop 'Safe Play' program guidelines.

The concept of safety requirements or 'Safe Play' guidelines are important for consideration in a school setting since the largest number of playground accidents and injuries occur during the first few weeks of a new school year. Thus, the safety week suggestion presented at the student council meeting became a September "Playground Safety Month" at Farley School. As a part of physical education classes, time was spent on each piece of playground apparatus, where students were challenged to explore various uses and the ways in which a piece of equipment could be used or abused. Also discussed were reasons why a school should have 'Safe Play' guidelines.

As a part of regular physical education activity, movement education lessons were presented where guided discovery or problem solving styles of teaching were employed. Through the use of these techniques, the children were encouraged to make decisions concerning safe use of the equipment. In the infrequent case that the child did not accept the responsibility for his own safe play, the teacher interacted with the child during these lessons to communicate what was or was not acceptable use of the apparatus. In this way it was possible to guide the students. The teacher or playground leader must be aware of the possibly hazardous areas of the playground (i.e. structures placed too close to each other causing dangerous pathways, specific poor design, or maintenance of structures. . .) to guide students in their choice of equipment and choice of activity for use on that equipment.

Following these structured activity sessions, the students discussed what they should and shouldn't do in order to play safely, to have fun, and to prevent accidents and injuries. It became obvious to the faculty working with the children during the use of this process, that in their expression of guidelines (e.g. "You can't. . . ; "Don't do. . .), the children had to be intentionally motivated to think in safe terms that were expressed positively.

Playground Guidelines

After exploration during motor activity and the discussions which followed, all 3rd, 4th, and 5th graders were asked to write at least 10 ideas (hereafter referred to as "10 Safety Ideas Written List") outlining what they thought were the most important guidelines for 'Safe Play' on Farley's playground. The purpose of this assignment was to move the children through the thinking process to the point where they would establish their own 'Safe Play' guidelines. The beauty of a technique that leads a student to this point in decision making is that a 'Safe Play' program can be customized for every particular school or play environment based on student input (see Table 4.1).

Table 4.1   Playground guidelines were generated by children from grades K—5 at Farley Elementary School.

Farley Elementary School Playground Guidelines

General

1   Play by the Golden Rule--treat others the way you want them to treat you. Be honest--practive good sportsmanship--share with others--be fair--be considerate. Don't fight!!
2. Stay in your own personal space while using equipment.
3. Try new things at your own risk and with the teacher's supervision. Learn new things slowly.
4. DO HAVE FUN!!!

Specific Behavior

5. Walk on the blacktop and on the gravel paths. You may move at your choice of speed on grass.
6. Don't throw rocks, sand, gravel, dirt, sticks.
7. Wear proper shoes and clothing--no loose clothing--tie your shoelaces--don't carry sharp objects in pockets.
8. Listen to the teachers and follow directions.
9. Always be with a friend or a buddy. Ask permission from the teacher before leaving the playground.

Maintenance

10. Take care of equipment and use it properly.
11. Report danger to the teacher (broken glass, sticks, broken equipment, snakes, strangers, dangerous play, etc.)

The first eleven guidelines have become Farley Elementary School playground guidelines. The students listed these guidelines most frequently in their "10 Safety Ideas Written List". They included in their guidelines, concerns like observing the golden rule, throwing objects, maintanence concerns and a buddy system.

The second set of guidelines (see Figure 4.2) were generated for specific pieces of equipment after exploratory play activity on each piece found on the Farley Elementary School playground. These guidelines were gathered from the "10 Safety Ideas Written List" mentioned above. The format for these guideline statements was more difficult to keep positive, as observation of Table 4.2 will show. It also becomes obvious after a review of Table 4.2 that Farley Elementary School playground is primarily populated with traditional playground equipment.

Table 4.2 Guidelines were generated by the students at Farley Elementary School for specific pieces of equipment.

GUIDELINES FOR SPECIFIC EQUIPMENT:

Swings
1. Don't jump out of high swings.
2. Swing properly--no bumpers, twists, flips, dives, climbs, doublerides.
3. Stay away from a swing in use.

Slide
1. Don't slide headfirst.
2. Don't walk up or down the slide.
3. One person on the slide at a time.

Climbing Equipment
1. Don't jump off of high places.
2. While climbing on equipment, keep three or more body parts touching the equipment at all times.
3. Don't stand under climbing equipment while others are using it.

Tunnel
1. Don't run through the tunnels.
2. No kissing in the tunnels!!!

Other suggestions for guidelines which grew from the "10 Safety Ideas Written List" are recorded here but were infrequently recorded on students' lists. They are presented to show the depth and the breadth of student concern for appropriate playground behavior (see Table 4.3). This is by no means an inclusive list but is presented here as an indicator of the freshness that only children's expressions can provide.

Table 4.3 Other guidelines which were not recorded as frequently, demonstrate the freshness of the children's approach to the 'Play Safe' program.

Other Rules Suggested By Students

1. Let the teacher know when you get sick!
2. Be calm when a snake bites you.
3. Don't jump in mud holes.
4. No biting or spitting.
5. Don't be foolish.
6. Don't swing a bat in a crowd.
7. Don't play in lightning.
8. Don't walk with your eyes closed.
9. Don't drink too much.
10. Don't run with anything in your mouth except your tongue or braces.
11. No kissing girls!!
12. Don't play near lawn-mowing tractors
13. Be aware of heat stress.
14. Don't talk to strangers.
15. Don't hide in the tall grass.
16. No 'whizzing' in the tunnels!

Poster Project

To insure continuation of concern about playground safety, a poster project was initiated at Farley Elementary School. The students in all grade levels were given an opportunity to make 'Safe Play' posters about their favorite playground guideline (see Figures

4.3 & 4.4). Student posters were placed on the walls in the most traveled hallways of the school. This practice set the stage for a re-emphasis of the 'Safe Play' program because students seem, by nature, to be interested in the artwork of others. An added advantage to this display procedure was that in many cases student illustrations were more easily understood by children than adult-designed illustrations. Thus, the students were reminded over and over again of the part that they play each day in their own safety.

Figure 4.3 The slide rule is shown.   Figure 4.4 The swing rule is shown

The poster theme of 'Safe Play' used in art lessons throughout the Farley Elementary School was but one of the most effective ways to keep the 'Safe Play' concept in front of the children. It should be noted that the attempt was made to include playground safety concepts in each of the following curriculum areas: 1) art, 2) health, 3) physical education, 4) reading, 5) English, 6) math, and 7) science (see Chapter 6). By emphasizing a connection in many curricular areas the curriculum blitz served to spike the interest level in all of the students (see Figure 4.5). It ran very high throughout the campaign. 'Safe Play,' in many ways, permeated the entire life thread of the school.

layground Safety Patrol

As suggested by the student council, a playground safety patrol as organized. The student playground safety patrol was a logical velopment when establishing safety on the playground and came a very important component of the entire 'Safe Play' progam. he responsibility of the playground safety patrol person was fined as providing assistance to the supervising teacher by onitering all playground activity.' That person for each week also as given the task of demonstrating adherence to established idelines in their own play. Ultimately, the patrol person's job came one of insuring that students adhered to student-generated fety guidelines.

The students policed the playground by approaching a student violation of established guidelines, and suggesting acceptable play ternatives to that student. This procedure worked successfully at e Farley Elementary school. As the students came to realize that ch of them would share the responsibility of being the safety trol person, little rejection of suggestions occurred.

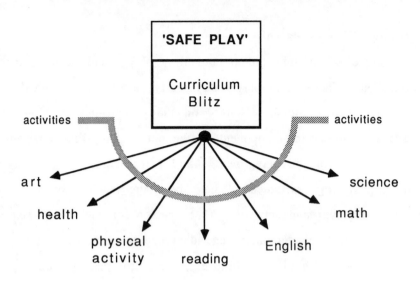

Figure 4.5 The 'Safe Play' curriculum blitz (see Chapter 6) included almost simultaneous participation in activities in most subjects taught in the school.

The Teacher's Role

These procedures and techniques associated with the 'Safe Play' program evolved from a set of natural occurrences. The student council representatives returned to the classrooms ready to use the expertise of the other students. The discussions that the student council representative lead in the classroom took the pressure off of the classroom teachers not directly involved in the organization of the program. Ultimately this was an important undertaking since it allowed the teachers the opportunity to observe the interactions and guide the process when necessary (see Chapter 5 for a more indepth discussion of one problem which may be encountered during teacher participation). In this manner the entire class remained active in the discussion and cognitively involved in its outcome.

At faculty meetings, teachers discussed the 'Safe Play' program and the legal responsibility of the supervising teacher or play leader. They were invited to the playground to better understand the reasons for guidelines. It was emphasized during these discussions that the play leaders should be visable and actively changing their position on the playground. This procedure was felt to be necessary to insure that the children were aware of, but not intimidated by their presence. The guidance provided by the play leader and received by the children was for the purpose of: 1) motivating the child to discover his/her capabilities and limitations, 2) helping the child develop a kinesthetic awareness of the demands of physical activity on the equipment, 3) stimulating interest and imagination in the child, 4) building confidence in the child, and 5) providing opportunities for responsible, considerate, and safe play behavior on the playground (see Figure 4.6).

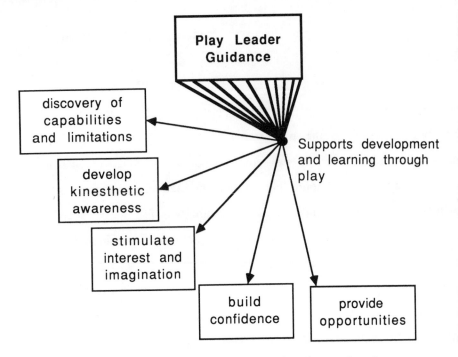

Figure 4.6 Play leaders provided guidance during play sessions for specific purposes.

The Objective of the 'Safe Play' Program

As a result the 'Safe Play' program at Farley Elementary School has been a positive, successful, joyous experience for all concerned. It is now an on-going, dynamic program, changing with the needs and designs of the students and faculty, and also with changes or improvements made in the play environment itself. The number one objective was then, and is now, to promote and preserve the child's right to safe play in both structured and unstructured settings (see Figure 4.7). In April, 1916, Harry Sperling wrote:

> The playground is essentially a place for play. . . Play gives health to the body and joy to the soul. Whoever has not tasted the pleasures of youth's playgrounds has missed much of the

sweetness of life. . . That which makes us laugh with unbounded joyousness and fills the heart with unselfish love helps to lubricate the wheels of altruism. . . [play] helps to enhance the joy of living.

As professionals who are responsible for educating children about safety during play, the challenge is to develop responsible, thinking young people. At the same time the immediate and overriding objective must be to provide safe, joyful living experiences in the environments provided for children.

'Safe Play' Program's #1 Objective

• **Promotion and Preservation of the Child's Right to Safe Play!**

Figure 4.7 Although the 'Safe Play' program is also concerned with accomplishing other objectives, the first objective remains the most important.

The potential for accomplishing this objective is through one of the greatest learning mediums - play. A 'Safe Play' program at Farley Elementary School made the initial impressions needed to accomplish this objective.

Bibliography

Bilbrough, A, & Jones, P. (1985). Physical education for the primary school. London: University of London Press LTD.

Brown, M.C. (1969). Movement Education: Its evolution and a modern approach. Reading MA: Addison -Wesley Pub. Co.

Kirchner, G., Cunningham, J., & Warrell, E. (1978). Introduction to movement education (3rd Ed.). Dubuque, IA: Wm C Brown Pub. Co.

Sperling, H. (1916). The playground book. New York: A. S. Barnes and Company.

CHAPTER 5

TEACHER COMMITMENT
TO PLAYGROUND SAFETY

by

L. D. Bruya
North Texas State University

The initiation of a student generated playground safety program on the school playground implies an involved process. To succeed at such an undertaking requires the combined efforts of an organizational leader and the teachers in the school. Unfortunately, many of the teachers in our schools are overwhelmed with the multiple needs of the children, complicated further by the demands of the state government for reports and paperwork. However, teacher support of the playground safety program is not only important but imperative if the program is to be successful.

Faculty Involvement

A carefully designed and well organized process must be undertaken to secure committed teacher involvement. This process, which is made up of a progression of small steps is used to convince teachers who are in many ways already overworked, of the need for playground safety process (referred to in Chapter 4 as the 'Safe Play' program), and school curriculum integration (see Chapter 6). It is apparent at the beginning of such an undertaking that even a

121

discussion in the classroom, which is the first step designed to involve children in the playground safety program, will not be successful unless the faculty is also involved in the concept of providing children the chance to control safety on the playground (see Figure 5.1).

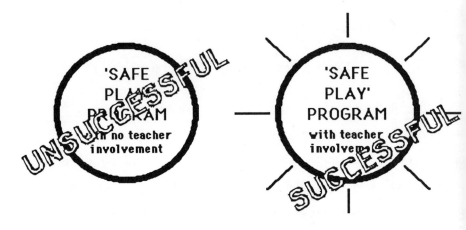

Figure 5.1 The involvement of the entire faculty rather than only one teacher in the playground safety insures its success.

The First Faculty Meeting. The faculty must be made aware of the plan to develop a playground safety program during a faculty meeting (usually the responsibility for organizing the explanation and the playground safety program falls to one interested faculty or a small core of teachers). Short explanation materials can be distributed to explain: 1) the need for the program, 2) the area within the school curriculum where playground safety instruction can take place, and that 3) the need for a curriculum integration is based on the concept of preventing and/or reducing injury while at the same time legally protecting the teachers and the school.

During the discussion which accompanies the materials presented in the faculty meeting, the organizational leader (frequently this person is the physical educator in the school) initiating the process which will lead to the playground safety program, should realize that teacher attitudes often change very slowly. This evolution is initially characterized by half interest, tacit approval, and then grows to an attitude characterized by committed involvement. The organizational leader may feel like he/she is "...never able to make progress," but headway must be measured in small changes and/or successes not in great leaps.

The organizational leader should understand that the committed involvement of teachers to a program for which they initially may not subscribe is a slowly evolving result of several progressive steps. These steps involved in the playground safety process include: 1) the initial faculty meeting (already discussed), 2) student council meetings, 3) curriculum integration, 4) classroom meetings, 5) informal faculty discussions, 6) gaining principal support, 7) an additional faculty meeting, 8) making a playground visitation, resulting in 9) the potential for changed playground supervision (see Figure 5.2).

Nine Steps
To Gain Teacher Committment

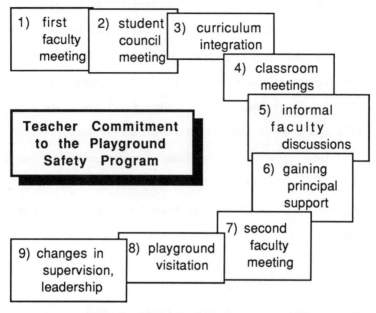

Figure 5.2   Developing teacher commitment to the playground safety program consists of nine steps.

The Student Council Meeting. It is not difficult to see that the concept of initiating a playground safety program through the student council has definite advantages for the organizational leader or teacher in charge. Most importantly, a strategy of this nature does not place additional responsibility on the regular classroom teacher for directing the development of the playground safety program. Low levels of responsibility, in which teachers are provided the opportunity to consider the idea of safety on the playground, provide time to reflect on the needs of the children and the role that each teacher might play in the playground safety program. Work loads related to supporting and guiding the students responsible for the playground safety program are assumed more easily following personal commitment. If the work load comes first, as a result of an assignment from those in a position of authority, teacher committment may never come.

In effect the teacher does not need to prepare materials or topics for the classroom discussion conducted by the student council representative. The teacher's responsibility during these discussions is simply to monitor the process as it takes place (see Figure 5.3). Through the limited need for initial involvement, the teacher is provided the opportunity to observe children as they struggle to control playground safety. The teacher need not assume responsibility for a successfully articulated playground safety program. Instead, the children can be expected to assume responsibility if the opportunity is provided. This is especially important since most teachers who are uncommitted to the concept of a playground safety program neither want to start one or know a whole lot about them.

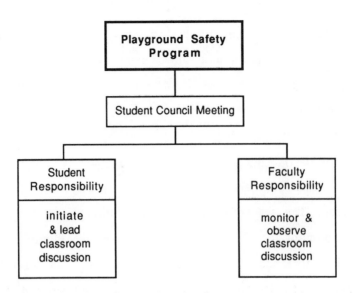

Figure 5.3 The initial responsibility for developing a playground safety program belongs to the student not the teacher.

A technique, leading to an increased teacher support for a child-controlled playground safety program is based on first increasing the strength and commitment of student involvement in the playground safety program. This is accomplished by developing excitement in the children in a manner similar to the way in which advertising on Saturday morning cartoons develops excitement for product lines.

In these advertisements children always seem to be in control of the toys with which they play and at the same time are free of adult supervision. The illusion of being free of adult supervision seems to add to a heightened effect of being in control. Together, these illusions provide a sense of ownership upon which the sales pitch is made. Potential ownership and the implication that children can exercise control over their parents by convincing their parents to

uy the toys for them, act together to sell the toy. In the same way,
hildren in the school understand the need for a playground safety
rogram and the fact that they are to be in control of and own the
rogram, the children will convince teachers of their role, just as
hildren convince parents to buy a toy (see Figure 5.4).

Playground Safety Process

Figure 5.4 As children get excited over controlling their own playground
safety program their enthusiasm and commitment helps
teachers make a similiar commitment.

However , the idea of children assuming contol of a school
sponsored program of such importance can be a concern to teachers.
To achieve the goal of student responsibility two steps need to be
aken: 1) teachers must be willing to assume a role of support and
guidance, and 2) a training program must be established for student
council members designed to prepare them for leadership roles (see
Figure 5.5)

Such a training program has been formulated in the Ysleta
Independent School District in El Paso, Texas (Bruya, 1987).   It is
discussed later in this chapter in the context of a process used by
eachers when attempting to develop student involvement in their
own playground safety guidelines.

127

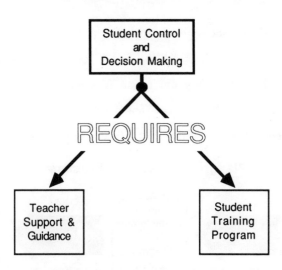

Figure 5.5 Teacher support and student training are required for responsible behavior in a playground safety program.

Curriculum Integration. The roots of the curriculum integration idea can be formed in the first student council meeting as the children themselves begin to struggle with the idea of the ways in which they can encourage the development of a playground safety program. As was demonstrated in Chapter 4, the responsibility for the initial discussions of a playground safety program and curriculum integration can occur in a student council meeting.

In Chapter 4, the art project, poster campaign, was shown to lead naturally to the idea of a including activities supporting safe play in other classroom subjects (see Figure 5.6). The concept of other related activities used in other parts of the curriculum became the definition for curriculum integration, the expansion of activities found in one part of the curriculum to other subjects (for examples and expansion of curriculum integration see Chapter 6). Although the idea of expanded playground safety activities can begin in

tudent council discussions, committed teachers always must assume
he final responsibility for planning the eventual integration.

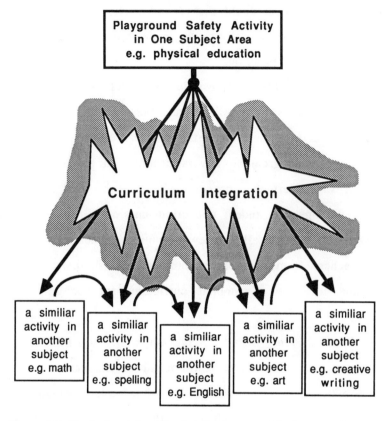

Figure 5.6 Curriculum integration begins as an activity in one subject
and is expanded into other areas.

Classroom Discussion.   The student council can serve
another valued function which can add significantly to the total
playground safety process.   Each member of the council must commit
himself/herself to the process of conducting a discussion in his/her
home classroom.   Each should understand that the support of the
other students is vital and must be cultivated in the classroom

discussion. As these discussions begin to occur, the teachers likely come to realize the strength of this process is that the people who intuitively know the most about playground safety - the children - are the ones who actually perform the leadership role in developing the playground safety program.

The playground safety process in the Ysleta Independent School District began with a well planned presentation by a single committed teacher (in this instance the physical educator) on a curriculum for the playground. Several teachers in the Ysleta schools in El Paso, Texas undertook a program which can be used as an example for the opening student council discussion (Bruya & Sommerfeld, 1987). Basically, a few committed educators (physical education teachers from different schools within the district) undertook and developed a complete curriculum for use on the playground.

The *Ysleta system* includes a procedure to assist in establishing student involvement and control of the safety program (see Figure 5.7). It was undertaken through a well articulated series of teaching techniques used to change attitudes of the children of the Ysleta school district. These same techniques, demonstrated in a student council meeting by an organizational leader, could prove helpful to student council members faced with the need to lead a discussion in their own classroom. The goal of the *Ysleta system* (here proposed for use by the student council members) was to increase the commitment and involvement of the students. The same goal is the basis for student led classroom discussions

130

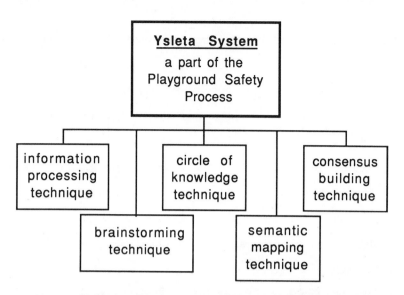

Figure 5.7 The Ysleta System consists of a series of techniques used in a sequence to train student council members for their role as leaders of classroom discussions and the playground safety program.

The *Ysleta system*, as outlined in the Ysleta materials (Bruya & Sommerfeld, 1987), includes a seven step progressive organization of individual techniques. Six of these techniques can be useful in the procedure used to train student council representatives for classroom discussion (see Figure 5.7). These techniques include: 1) information processing, 2) brainstorming, 3) circle of knowlege using words, 4) semantic mapping (Johnson, Pittleman & Heimlich, 1986), 5) reapplication of the circle of knowlege using concepts, and 6) consensus building (Alverez, Hernandez & Meraz, 1986). When the *Ysleta system*, which is used to solicit playground safety guidelines and thereby change attitudes, is explained as a part of a training process for student council members, natural enthusiasm and confidence, helps student council members succeed in the classroom discussion.

During the first student council meeting, formulating a plan of attack for increasing student involvement is important to eventual success. As the teachers watch excitement grow in the students , some are pulled into the classroom discussions lead by the student council member. Since many teachers possess organizational skills, they are able to help provide the structure which is needed to conduct the curriculum integration process and the growth of a playground safety program.

Informal Teacher Discussions. Usually, after observing discussions lead by student council members, and observing the student commitment which is its result, some of the teachers begin to be involved on their own. One or two excited ones begin talking about the playground safety program in informal discussion settings; in the faculty lounge during lunch or before/after school, in the cafeteria during lunch monitoring, on the playground during recess or in the teacher workroom during class preparation and planning periods. Other faculty may hear and perceive their growing excitement and commitment. In this way additional teachers begin to be involved themselves. In other words the news spreads from the student council to the classroom and from a few teachers in the classroom to other teachers in their informal discussions (see Figure 5.8). Many of the teachers in the school can be lead to commit their time and their energy to the playground safety program and the curriculum integration process.

However, there will also likely be a few who will not become involved. To make the process work and accomplish the goal of establishing a playground safety program it is ussually wise to involve negative attitude teachers as little as possible. It is wise to base the faculty support process on those teachers who most strongly support the program.

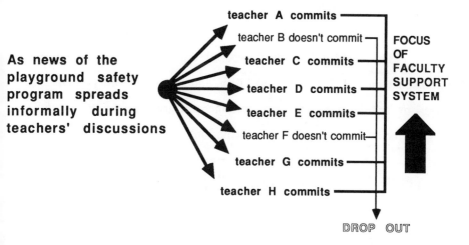

As news of the playground safety program spreads informally during teachers' discussions

teacher A commits
teacher B doesn't commit
teacher C commits
teacher D commits
teacher E commits
teacher F doesn't commit
teacher G commits
teacher H commits

FOCUS OF FACULTY SUPPORT SYSTEM

DROP OUT

Figure 5.8 The news of the playground safety program can spread through informal discussions to involve many of the teachers in the school.

Principal Support. Of course it is both necessary and wise if the teacher masterminding the process of establishing the playground safety program communicates directly and on a regular basis with the the school principal. If the principal is convinced of the worth of the program1, and he/she communicates that conviction to the faculty through example, it will help convince teachers of the need for commitment to the safety program.

The Second Faculty Meeting. After a period in which informal discussions between teachers are likely to occur, the organizing teachers' next step is to establish an adgenda item for the next faculty meeting through the principal. This second faculty meeting becomes the next vehicle for expanding teacher commitment to the playground safety program (see Figure 5.9).

But, the discussions change. Teachers begin to understand where the program is heading, and share the enthusiasm of the students. The faculty becomes involved during their own meetings with discussions of legal responsibility and school liability related to injuries or accidents which occur on the playground (see Figure 5.9 and Chapter 10 for additional information).

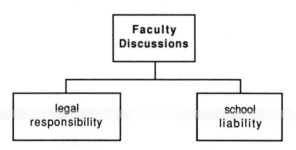

Figure 5.9 Faculty discussions frequently center upon legal responsibility and school liability.

Playground Visitation. A well placed comment by the organizational leader suggesting that all faculty might physically go to the playground itself, is usually met with approval. After all of the preparations outlined above, teachers appear ready to undertake a fresh look at the playground for the purpose of better understanding: 1) the potential problems, 2) the need for the rogram, and 3) the ways of including discussions and activities oncerning the playground safety program in other classroom subject reas.

Through growing personal concern and commitment, teachers egin to understand the need for the guidelines that the students are ttempting to develop through student council and classroom meetings. As they understand more about the need for and the development of the structure of the program, their involvement and ommittment also grows.

Playground Supervision—Play Leadership. It becomes more apparent to teachers that their job as the playground upervisor, with all of its hidden responsibilties, should be taken with more active interest. As a normal course of events, faculty members come slowly to understand that their behavior must change to provide better for the safety of children. Thus, the re-examination of the responsibilities of the playground supervisor, and he emphasis on child controlled safety processes lead to the onclusion that the supervisor is there to assist and guide children. The concept of adult assistance provided during play is more closely ligned with the idea of play leadership than play supervision.

To provide assistance and to actively support the play patterns of children, teachers may decide that play leaders need to be moving ontinually on the playground to monitor occurances; or at the very east play leaders should be visible to the majority of the players at all times. In this and other ways faculty may decide that supervision or leadership behavior on the playground must be redefined.

Some faculty arrive at the conclusion that the play leader should become more involved in playground activities by attempting to stimulate interest or imagination through suggested activities[2]. In this way faculty begin to see the potential of the playground session as containing the opportunity to reinforce skills taught in other curriculum areas. Supervisors begin to be seen as playleaders who help shape responsible and safe behavior on the playground.

Thus, the most difficult task of educating the teachers is complete. Teachers can be lead quite naturally to involvement with the playground safety process and eventually to changing their own behavior on the playground. Of course, none of this process can occur without the involvement and the excitement of the students. It is the foundation upon which the safety program is built.

End Notes

1. The principal can be most easily persuaded of the importance of the playground safety program if he/she is engaged in an organized discussion about school liability. An outline of an argument concerning liability and the risks involved in maintaining a school playground facility may be found in the last chapter of this text (see Chapter 10).

2. The Ysleta Outdoor Learning Environment *Project OLE'* playground curriculum guide is one such example of the work teachers have completed when they have become interested in the activities which occur on the playground during play.

Bibliography

Bruya, L.D. (1987). The development of attitudes related to the reduction of injury for the outdoor learning environment (Project OLE'). In L.D. Bruya and D. Sommerfeld (Eds.), Project OLE': An essential elements curriculum for use in the outdoor learning environment. El Paso, TX: Ysleta Independent School District.

Bruya, L.D. & Sommerfeld, D. (Eds.). (1987). Project OLE': An essential elements curriculum for use in the outdoor learning environment. El Paso, TX: Ysleta Independent School District.

Alvarez, R., Hernandez, T. & Meraz, D. (1986). Instructional Strategies: Department of elementary education, Ysleta I.S.D. El Paso. TX: Ysleta Independent School District.

Johnson, D.D., Pittleman, S. D. & Heimlich, J.E. (April 1986). Semantic Mapping. The Reading Teacher, pp. 778-782.

CHAPTER 6

A SYSTEM TO ESTABLISH
PLAYGROUND SAFETY IN THE SCHOOL

b y

E. Warrell
Simon Fraser University

The results of the survey of elementary school playground equipment (Bruya & Langendorfer, in press) indicate that our elementary school playgrounds are in trouble. If the concept of our neighborhood elementary school playground is to be preserved, it is apparent that public awareness needs to be raised concerning safety principles and practices. Increased knowledge of the cause of accidents and increased action designed to decrease the frequency of accidents must be the major concerns of a campaign to educate those involved in playgrounds.

An educational campaign designed to teach others about playgrounds is best articulated in the elementary schools where heavy playground use occurs. For children, playgrounds have always been associated with fun and new challenges, many of which require courage as well as skill. The question which must be answered prior to planning a program to improve playground safety is, "Do we, as adults, prepare children to play, have fun, and gain courage?" Or, "Do we forbid them to use equipment in certain ways or leave them in ignorance to learn by trial and error? Do we neglect to provide safe opportunities and encourage responsible decision making?"

Although answers to these questions will not of themselves resolve the issue of assisting children to play safely, they should serve to awaken us to the sense of responsibility which we share. That responsibility is to prepare children to make prudent decisions which will keep them safe during play.

Unfortunately, as is often the case, we unnecessarily regiment our children during their first school experiences. The appearance of order and systematic organization can lead to a false sense of safety. It can happen quite innocently and without intention by the instructor (see Figure 6.1). In fact, many times *the instructor may even conclude that they are encouraging safety during play through teacher control and regimentation.*

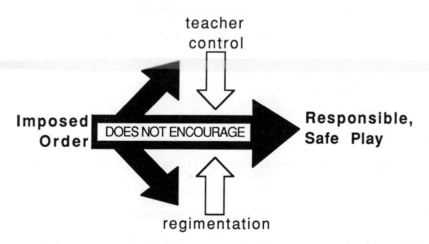

Figure 6.1 Responsible play behavior is not encouraged by imposed order based on teacher control and regimentation.

Kindergarten children enter the classroom and are encouraged
r even taught to sit in a circle. It may take the entire lesson or even
everal days but the children soon learn that circle sitting is
ewarded by the teacher. Through inference, the circle becomes the
est way to behave in class, leads to the fewest conflicts with
achers, and is safer since fewer occurrences of conflict develop.

Then as children begin to move, say in the gymnasium, they
re encouraged or assume that running or moving about the
ymnasium in a circle is safest since fewer confrontations with
thers occur. This is a misleading assumption. Children are lulled
to a false sense of safety and, after several repetitions of the same
ctivity, progressively pay less attention to what they are doing
hen running in a circle. Of course being less attentive during play
nd activity is counter productive to the concept of safe play (see
igure 6.2).

As small variations in the pattern used while moving in a circle
egin to occur and children begin simultaneously to be less attentive
 the environment, small accidents do begin to occur, even though
hildren running in a circle should not bump each other. However,
e reality is that they do bump and have accidents. The problem is
at the responsibility for the bump never seems to be the problem
f the bumper. Instead the responsibility for the bump is deferred
 someone else. This may occur because the children come to
redict the movements required of circle running. Then when the
attern changes, they bump. They do not assume responsibility for
eir own actions since they were doing as they were told and
erforming in predictable ways. In this manner adults, unwittingly

encourage irresponsible behavior in the very children in whom we are attempting to develop a sense of responsibility (see Figure 6.2).

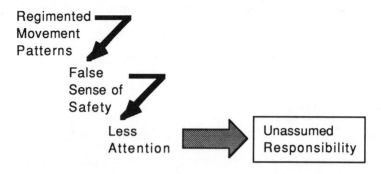

Figure 6.2 Teachers may unwittingly foster irresponsible behavior through regimentation.

An alternate example of the opening lesson in a gymnasium will provide a better understanding of one way in which more responsible behavior might be encouraged. Let's assume that the space in which the class will move is slightly larger than the regular classroom which just accomodates the children. If we ask them to run in this space while they "change directions every few steps. . . " a different running pattern occurs.

They practice running slowly at first and only increase their speed as their ability, skill, and need for safer movement allow. They change direction, they move into empty space. They begin to do the very things that will likely keep them safe during other subsequent lessons. There may still be bumps or other small accidents but the children are prepared and attentive and this allows them to recover without injury. In addition, they know intuitively, if it isn't explained by the teacher beforehand, that the bumps and falls are as much their fault as the other since it could have been avoided

f: 1) they had moved more slowly, 2) watched better, or 3) just
plain paid more attention.

The problem with most of our techniques in the school is that
we do not trust children to make decisions which are safe (see Figure
6.3). We do not expect them to think for themselves or use their
natural protective processes which would prevent them from
attempting activities beyond their ability. We design programs that
provide false senses of safety and in the process lessen the natural
occurrence or chance to act responsibly.

WE DO NOT TRUST CHILDREN TO MAKE DECISIONS ABOUT THEIR OWN SAFETY!

Figure 6.3 Educators may design regimented programs because
they don't trust children.

However, there is much that can be done to prevent accidents
and save our playgrounds from the rising cost of playground
litigation. Responsible and skilled behavior can be encouraged in our
children and result in saved lives and fewer injuries. A program of
playground safety can and should be undertaken in every school.
This program could cross all subjects and provide the student with
the opportunity to make responsible decisions about playing safely,
while increasing their knowledge and changing their attitudes
toward safe play.

Integrated Playground Safety Process

The concept of responsible behavior on the playground is best developed as a result of multiple activities which occur in several of the subjects taught in the school. Treated as a theme, the topic of playground safety can eventually permeate all subject areas (see Figure 6.4). What follows is a subject by subject consideration of activities which could be used to support the concept of playing safely on the playground.

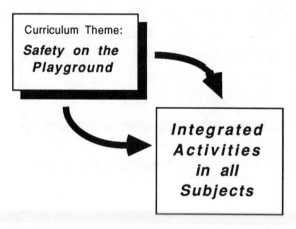

Figure 6.4 The theme of safety on the playground can be used to encourage activities in all curriculum areas.

Physical Education Activities. The curriculum area incorporated in physical education lends itself almost perfectly to the study of safety on the playground. Following is a list of several ideas which could be included in physical education.

1. Take the class to the playground and have children find all possible movements that they could do on each piece of equipment (or on each event).

2. Discuss the activities generated for each piece of equipment and decide which are safe and which might lead to injury.

3. Provide safety training related to the use of space in the gym (Kirchner, Cunningham & Warrell, 1977).

4. Provide safety training related to the use of a safety roll (Kirchner et al.).

5. Provide instruction in skill themes (Gabbard, LaBlanc & Lowy, 1987) on playground equipment.

Language Arts Activities. The language arts curriculum lends itself to the development of guidelines for responsible behavior on the playground. Following are activities which could be included in the language arts curriculum.

1) Begin a discussion in which children formulate their own guidelines1 for responsible playground behavior. Ask the children to write the guidelines as if they were teaching their younger brother or sister.

2) After the first draft has been completed, discuss the reasoning behind each guideline. Also discuss the need for writing the guidelines using positive language. Undertake the task of rewriting all guidelines which are not positive and active (e.g. guideline: "When climbing a piece of equipment be sure to keep three body parts in contact with the equipment at all times.")

3) Encourage children to vote on and select the ten most valuable guidelines proposed by their class. Then suggest that each child rewrite the guidelines using their best handwriting. Select guideline copies for:

    a. the safety council-Safety Journal

b. for display on the classroom notice board

c. for display in the hallway outside the classroom.

4) Write an essay on the following topics:

a. "A Playground Adventure",

b. "What Can I Do To Make The Playground A Safer Place?",

c. "What The Double Wide Slide Said To The Fire Pole!"

5) Submit selected essays to the Safety Journal.

6) Develop safety crossword puzzles and submit them to the Safety Journal.

7. Develop safety riddles or jingles and submit them to the Safety Journal.

Fine Arts Activities. Activities included as a part of the language arts curriculum can be used to graphically display guidelines for responsible behavior on the playground. What follows are a few examples of these activities.

1) Discuss the concept and use of the poster to advertise safety on the playground.

2) Discuss magazine cover art using current magazines found on the newstand. Encourage children to develop and submit their ideas of cover art to be used for the Safety Journal.

3) Use the playstructures found on the school playground as sources for still life drawings and/or paintings.

4) Encourage drawings of potential accidents which might occur on the playground.

5) Provide magazines to clip photos and develop a collage of non-sensical accidents which might occur on the playground.

Science Activities. Scientific principles can be used to describe the force of a fall or explain why a fall actually occurs. The activities selected for use in the science curriculum could demonstrate these principles. A few examples of these activities are listed below.

1) Examine the concept of gravity as a way of predicting when falls will ocur as different body positions are assumed on the play structure.

2) Examine techniques to absorb force during landing or during falls from playground equipment.

3) Examine the principle and encourage a written description of the part played by a stable base of support while using a part of the playground equipment.

4) Examine acceleration rates over graduated distances related to the height of the playground equipment and write a report concerning height and its potential effect upon the safety of players.

5) Discuss gravity and encourage a written description of the part played by the concept of acceleration which increases the force of a fall.

Math Activities. There are numerous opportunities for students to use measurement techniques to collect information about the structures on the school playground. Listed below are several of the activities which could be used as a part of a math unit.

1) Make a scale model of the existing equipment on the playground.

2) Using the Consumer Product Safety Commission guidelines listed in their publications (USCPSC, 1980a; 1980b), compare the

147

suggested sizes and distances between equipment, to the sizes and distances actually occurring between equipment on the school playground.

3) Measure and record the heights of all likely sites of a fall.

4) Calculate the expenditure of funds used to place the current equipment on the playground. Calculate the percentage of tax needed and add it to the total.

5) Select equipment from catalogues currently available on the market and calculate the cost of replacing the current playground structure with new and updated versions. Calculate the expense of installation (44%) and containment walls and safety ground cover (20%-40%) and arrive at the total estimated expense for a new playground. Submit this calculation to the PTA along with a request for a campaign to finance a new playground.

6) Measure and record sample depths of the safety surface placed under the structure and calculate average or mean depth.

7) Measure all angles of intersection for structural parts found on the playground and determine which angles hold the potential for entrapment (see USCPSC, 1980a).

Social Studies Activities. The social studies curriculum provides multiple opportunities to examine the school playground. Listed below are several of the ideas that could be used to reflect that curriculum.

1) Conduct a survey of local park playground equipments and compare that survey to one of the elementary school playground.

2) Conduct a project in which records are kept of all social behaviors as groups of children play on the playground structures.

ubmit the results of the survey to the Safety Council for publication n the Safety Journal.

3) Read selected literature from the adventure playground 1ovement and determine how adventure playgrounds create a ifferent social setting than do traditional playgrounds.

4) Prepare a survey of parents' attitudes and memories of 1eir childhood playground. Record these memories and compare 1em to. . .

       a.   what is currently available on the playground

     _ b.   what is currently available on the market.

5) Using the library, research playgrounds in other countries nd list similiarities and differences between them.

he Safety Council Concept

The elementary school safety council is one technique which an be used to emphasize playground safety in the school. The dvantages of using a technique of this type are fourfold (see Figure 5). First, a safety council which meets regularly for the purpose of 1creasing safety in the school and particularly on the playground is kely to keep the concept fresh in the minds of children and teachers ike. Second, electing a safety council reflects on the need for 2mocratic rule and provides a chance for children to gain first hand 1perience in the process. Third, control and ownership of a ayground safety program run by the safety council remains in the 1nds of the children with guidance provided by the teachers in the hool. Fourth, in case of accident, and occasional related liability it, the safety council and its educational processes can be used as part of the plan of defense (Bruya & Beckwith, 1985: see chapter on risk)

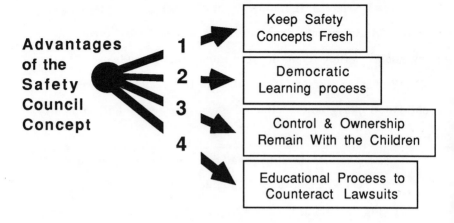

Figure 6.5 The safety council can be used to support a playground safety program.

Composition of the Safety Council.   Membership should be elected by the children as part of the initiation of the playground safety program.   The size of the council depends partially on the size of the school and other factors.   General guidelines for a Safety Council in any school are shown in Table 6.1.

Table 6.1 Guidelines for establishing a safety council are similiar when applied in any size school.

Guidelines for Safety Council Membership

- 12 grade six children
- 2 children from each class (K-6)
  2 Teachers selected from those proposed
  by the teachers
- 2 Parents selected from those proposed
  by the parents
- principal & janitor as non-elected members

Grade six students should chair the meetings and work out the agenda for each meeting. The sixth grade students in a normal elementary school setting probably should assume the primary reponsibility for conducting the program, producing the journal, and initiating the safety patrol (principal and teachers should be involved in guidance capacities only).

Safety Council Responsibilities. All elected members of the safety council should share in the responsibility for the decision making process. Prior to major decisions each member should return to their classroom to explain upcoming decisions to their class members. In this way they can collect information from their constituency prior to decisions. Thus, the representative nature of their position will be maintained (see Figure 6.6).

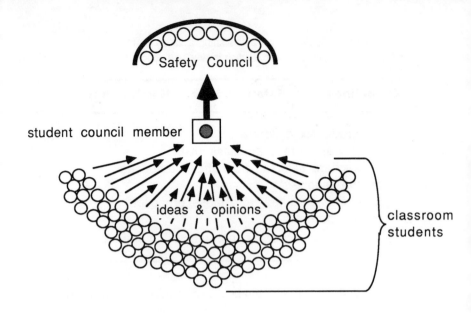

Figure 6.6 Each council member has the responsibility to represent the ideas and opinion of those who elected him/her.

Other responsibilities for the safety council include involvement in all parts of the playground safety program. Some of these responsibilities are listed below:

1. Safety Guidelines: To formulate and implement a positive safety program for the whole school;

2. Judging: To act as adjudicators for selection of essays and posters submitted for publication in the Safety Journal;

3. Safety Patrol: To organize a duty roster consisting of 4 representatives (2 grade six + 2 from another grade level) to patrol the playground at recess and noon hour and to check equipment and encourage safe behaviors (e.g. emphasize positive guidelines; regulate number on each piece of equipment. . .);

4. Safety Reports: To gather regular reports from the custodian on the condition of the equipment;

5. Maintenance: To determine what children can do to keep equipment and the playground in good condition;

6. Equipments: To develop a set of behavior expectations for each piece of equipment to provide these expectations for each patrol duty officer.

The Safety Journal

The Safety Journal can be initiated by and support provided by the Safety Council. At the time of etablishing the Safety Journal staff the frequency of publication can be determined as well as the purpose and objectives for the ...Journal. Essays and art works which are generated by the activities suggested for units in langauge arts, science, math, and social studies, could be used for the content of the ..Journal. Parents,Teachers, and especially children from all of the grades should be encouraged to submit works to the ...Journal for publication.

Purpose and Objectives. The purpose for using the journal concept is to provide a format for the ordered consideration of ways in which to improve safety on the playground (see Figure 6.7).

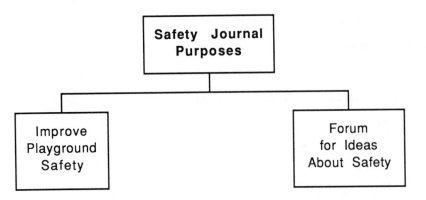

Figure 6.7 The Safety Journal used as a part of the school safety program is based upon two purposes.

The secondary purpose is to provide a format which can be conrolled by the children and will act as a forum for their written and drawn ideas about safety.

To accomplish these purposes the journal tasks might be divided to reflect the objectives listed below:

1) collect, select and prepare essays and articles about safety

2) collect, select and prepare art work about safety

3) collect, select and prepare cover art work

4) collect, select and prepare puzzles, jingles and stories about safety.

The two tasks that must be accomplished related to these objectives are: a) publication of safety ideas, and b) solicitation of safety ideas.

Soliciting Safety Ideas. Safety ideas can be solicited by regularly asking teachers for ideas developed by the children about safety. Collection of art work and articles could be accomplished in the same way through the same process.

The Safety Council may also wish to undertake a short Newsletter' to the teachers designed to outline a curriculum idea of the month concerning safety. The simplest way to do this would be to suggest one activity for use in each curriculum area for each month. In this way interest in the concept of playground safety could be kept alive during each month of the nine month school year (see Figure 6.8).

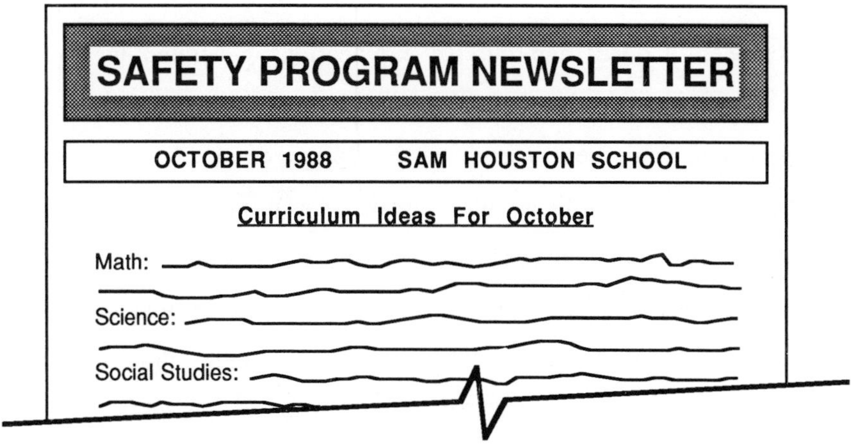

SAFETY PROGRAM NEWSLETTER

OCTOBER 1988   SAM HOUSTON SCHOOL

Curriculum Ideas For October

Math:

Science:

Social Studies:

Figure 6.8 The Newsletter can provide teachers with new safety program ideas for use in the curriculum each month.

Publication of Safety Ideas. Publication of articles and art work about safety requires first that materials be readily available for publication. To insure that materials are readily available it is necessary that an organized effort be made to collect safety materials. These materials should probably reflect the activities which are taking place in the classroom from all of the curriculum areas. Following are some of the article ideas which might be collected from teachers who conducted playground safety activities in the different classroom curriculum areas:

• Physical Education: Collect and publish lists of movements which could be executed on each piece of playground equipment.

• Language Arts: Collect and publish, by grade levels, lists of guidelines for activities on the playground. Publish essays written about playgrounds and safety and about whimsical topics related to playgrounds.

• Science: Collect and publish explanations generated by children concerning the cause of increased force of impact from various heighted equipment found on the playground.

• Mathematics: Collect and publish measurements, heights and dimensions of all equipment on the playground. Publish estimates of the cost of current structures on the playground and estimates of the expense of replacing current structures with updated equipment.

• Social Studies: Publish surveys of currently available equipment found on other school playgrounds and in the parks within the general area of the school. Publish reports on the total resources available for play for elementary school children within the general school area. Publish essays on the social benefits of playgrounds and the unique contribution which the adventure playground concept can make to children.

• Fine Arts: Collect and publish designs for the cover of the Safety Journal (see Figure 6.9). Publish drawings and other art work depicting accidents and ways in which they can be avoided.

Safety Journal
Clement Elementary School

Figure 6.9 The cover of each Safety Journal could depict art work submitted for publication by one of the children in the school.

These ideas only provide a brief outline of the many ideas which may occur as a result of activities teachers present in the classroom when they begin to use the newsletter curriculum ideas circulated to them by the safety council. With the support of the teachers and principal in the school many additional materials could be available for publication in the Safety Journal.

Safety Journal Staffing. For the most part the journal staff should be comprised of sixth grade council members and a smaller contingency of fifth grade students. Fifth grade student staff members serve a dual function: first, as productive staff members, and second, as a transitional group needed to lead the next year's journal.

The position that each member fills could be assigned by a student editor-in-chief. The positions may only include responsibility for information grouped in ways which reflect the objectives listed above or responsibility may also include photography, grade correspondent, advertising, printing and/or distribution.

Playground Safety Program Support

Each person involved in the school program either directly as in the case of principals, teachers and children, or peripherally as in the case of parents, can demonstrate support for the concept of playground safety through a series of behaviors (see Figure 6.10). If the program is going to succeed it is necessary that all of the people involved in the program support it in some way. To give examples of the way in which the safety program can be supported by the people involved in the school, the following lists of guidelines are presented.

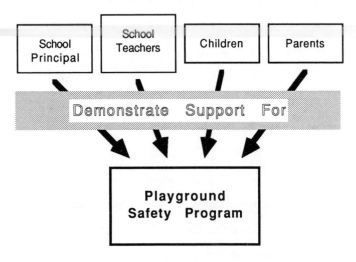

Figure 6.10   Persons involved in the school can demonstrate their support of the Playground Safety Program.

Guidelines for Principals.

1. Set a date for a 'Safety Week' in September or early October.

2. Set up elections for safety council members to take place on the first day of 'Safety Week.'

3. Provide an opportunity for teacher and parent inservice programs held during September and October.

4. Reinforce positive playground behavior on many occasions throughout the year broadcasting over the P.A. system and posting a weekly accident record by class/by school outside the main office.

Guidelines for Teachers.

1. Attend inservice sessions to become acquainted with the safety techniques being taught in the Physical Education unit. Review and use suggested activities in language arts, math, science, social studies and art that may be implemented during year.

2. Nominate and propose several teachers willing to be involved in the school safety council.

3. Organize the election of two children to represent their class on the safety council.

4. While using curriculum materials designed to promote playground safety establish an assignment which will involve both the parent and the child in the safety process.

5. On your playground duty day, insure that the safety patrol is functioning properly by helping them to organize at the beginning of the play period.

6. Personally reinforce positive safety behavior on the playground rather than dwelling on rule breakers.

7. Coordinate children's art work, articles and essays submitted to the safety council and Safety Journal.

8. Display the children's work generated during various playground safety activities in the classroom, in the hallways and even in shopping malls if arrangements can be made.

Guidelines for Parents.

1. Reinforce positive playground safety behaviors (e.g. 1. "Only try things that you feel comfortable trying." 2. "Hold on with both hands; reach with your toes.").

2. Encourage your child to use the lower equipment first since falls which might occur will be less lethal.

3. Encourage balancing, jumping, and landing while playing on low equipment.

4. Refrain from encouraging play on high equipment. Children will progress to this equipment naturally as they are ready to handle the potential of falling from it.

5. Encourage climbing down from equipment hand over hand and gripping with the feet to control speed and prevent sliding.

6. Allow plenty of time for play activity.

7. Avoid lifting the child onto or off equipment.

8. Expect that some cildren will move more quickly than others.

9. Avoid comparisons between children.

10. Expect that some children will be more adventurous than others.

11. Contribute your ideas to the school program.

12. Seek information on safety techniques.

13. Discuss the responsibility for safety and safe play with your child.

Guidelines for Children.

1. Assume responsibility for your own safety.

2. Formulate guidelines which will govern playground play.

3. Elect representatives to the school safety council.

4. Sign a declaration stating that you will adhere to the rules.

5. Take responsibility for reporting broken or damaged equipment to the custodian or person responsible for repairs.

6. Understand all the rules used to govern the playground.

7. Serve on the safety council if asked.

8. Participate as a member of the safety patrol if asked.

9. Act responsibly at all times.

10. Be kind and considerate when playing on the playground.

Though these suggested behaviors outline some of the possible ways that the playground safety program can be supported in the school they will not insure its success. Even the formation of a safety council in which children act responsibly to control safety on the playground, or the development of a Safety Journal, used to elucidate points about safety, will not insure the playground safety program's success.

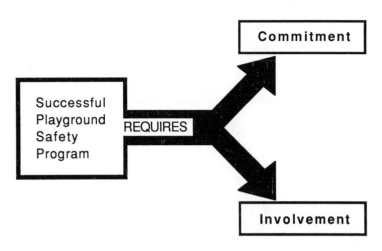

Figure 6.11 A Safety Journal, A Newsletter of even a safety council cannot insure the success of the playground safety program without commitment and the willingness to be involved.

To be successful, the program must become a part of the very fiber of the school and a part of the makeup of each individual involved in the school. Personal commitment and the involvement of each teacher, parent and child in an educational process related to safety is required (see Figure 6.11). These occur through daily cultivation of concern for others and regular consideration for how safe play can affect what children learn and how they develop. To this end these ideas are presented.

End Notes

1. Refer to the discussion of the *Ysleta System* in Chapter 7.

Bibliography

Bruya, L. D. & Langendorfer, S. J. (Eds.). (In Press). Where our children play: Elementary school Playground Equipment. Washington, DC: AAHPERD, AALR-COP.

Bruya, L. D. & Beckwith, J. (Winter, 1985). Due process: Reducing exposure to liability suits and the management of risk associated with children's play areas. Children's Environments Quarterly, 2 (4), 29-35.

Gabbard, C., LeBlanc, E. & Lowy, S. (1987). Physical education for children: Building the foundation. Englewood Cliffs, NJ: Prentice-Hall, Inc.

Kirchner, G., Cunningham, J. & Warrell, E. (1970). Introduction to movement education. Dubuque, IA: Wm. C. Brown Co. Pub.

U. S. Consumer Product Safety Commission (1980a). A handbook for public playground safety (Vol. I. General guidelines for new and existing playgrounds). Washington, D. C.: U. S. Government Printing Office.

U. S. Consumer Product Safety Commission (1980b). A handbook for public playground safety (Vol. II.: Technical guidelines for equipment and surfacing). Washington, D. C.: U. S. Government Printing Office.

PART THREE:

Current
Playground Solutions
For Children

CHAPTER 7

PROJECT OLE`:
OUTDOOR LEARNING ENVIRONMENT
FOR CHILDREN

submitted by

D. Sommerfeld & C. Dunn
Ysleta Independent School District
El Paso, Texas

With the advent of the 1984 educational reform legislation in the state of Texas the Ysleta Independent School District (ISD) in El Paso engaged in a comprehensive review of its total instructional program. As an integral part of this process, all classroom and specialty curriculums were examined. The examination of the physical education curriculum and the playgrounds on which the activities were held led to the evaluation of the play structures which were present at that time.

It was apparent during this review process that existing playground equipment was serving more of a recreational than instructional purpose. After several discriminating observations, it became obvious that the existing equipment was providing activity only for a small group of the children who were available to use it. It was determined that curriculum designed to use a standardized system of equipment would be beneficial for the development of all children in the school district. This examination process and curriculum evaluation lead to a program of equipment and curriculum improvements.

The Initiation of Project OLE`

A district wide committee was organized to explore the issue of the educational use of the playground and the direction that the outdoor play equipment improvements should take. Current trends in playground equipment design (Bruya, 1985; see chapter 10) and the implication for integration of that equipment into the physical education instructional program were examined (Dauer and Pangrazi, 1986; Kirchner, 1985; Logsdon, Barrett, Broer, McGee, Ammons, Halverson and Roberton, 1984).

A sub-committee composed of an elementary school principal, an elementrary school physical education teacher and the Ysleta ISD supervisor for physical education was formed. The committee made on-site observations of playground apparatus at over 20 locations. These locations included public schools, private schools, churches, and daycare centers.

At each location the same questions were asked during interviews of site supervisors.

1. "What type of problems are evident with the play apparatus on this location?"
2. "Do the children prefer one part of the equipment over others?"
3. "Does the vendor from whom the structure was purchased provide follow-up service?"
4. "If the purchase could be redone, would the same type of equipment and manufacturer be selected for purchase again?"

Answers to these questions and other information acquired during the interview and observation process were recorded. The information helped Ysleta ISD administrators and teachers focus on the relative effectiveness of the play structures and to address potential problems with types of equipment or manufactures prior to purchase.

Uniquenesses of the Ysleta Setting

During the evaluation period which followed the observations, construction materials and structure details were assessed for application potential within the Ysleta ISD. This became a major concern of the committee since the Ysleta school playgrounds and the El Paso area are unique in several ways. First of all, the soil in most of the schools is the type found in the desert. It is sandy and frequently hard packed due to the parched nature of the climate. Second, since little rain occurs in the El Paso area and drainage is not a problem, safety surface pits under the structures were feasible (see chapter 3). Third, the constant sun and relatively high air temperature increase the likelihood of burns from hot metal during play. Fourth, much of the physical education instructional curriculum takes place on the playground.

A Comprehensive Proposal.

These characteristics of the area, and the interview /observation process, helped to shape the committees' thoughts and eventual recommendations. A comprehensive proposal was prepared and presented to the board of trustees for the school district. In the proposal the board was particularly interested in the otential for use of the environment for instructional purposes. As a esult, their response was positive, enthusiastic, and unanimous. They indicated that the district could proceed and, in fact, should "Go or it!"

The process of establishing quality play structures on the playgrounds of the Ysleta school district began to pick up momentum. A model which included posts, platforms and play events (Beckwith, 1985) was constructed which reflected current design. Particular events were selected because they were felt to be essential to the development of the children who would use them, and because they would fit the physical education curriculum.

The Design Of The OLE` Structure

The system was based on an interconnected design (Shaw, 1976), was rich with stimulating and challenging events (Beckwith, 1985; Frost & Klein, 1979), was modular in nature (Frost & Klein, 1979), and highly complex (Bruya, 1979; Beckwith, 1985). Minor design modifications and variations were included even as construction was taking place. As a result, each school in the Ysleta ISD was in a position to receive a standardized playground structure which provided the potential for cross discipline curriculum integration. The project became known as Project OLE' (Outdoor Learning Environment).

Outdoor Learning Environment

Following approval by the Ysleta school board, the purchasing process was initiated. Eventually this process culminated in the largest single purchase of playground equipment in the history of the playground equipment industry: $600,000.00.

About two months passed between the initial order and the installation of the first structure. To increase involvement in the process and to heighten anticipation at each of the schools, the principals and schools' faculties prepared lists of all available equipment currently on their playgrounds. The principals ranked the lists by quantity of apparatus and determined that the schools most deficent in equipment would be the first to receive a new structure. They also assessed the need for retaining some of the currently available equipment and made requests for removal or repair of all others. Within one year, a complete system was installed at each campus in the district.

From the beginning and throughout the past two years since installation began, the children have seemed to be attracted to the yellow and orange ladders, slides and tunnels. They like the excitement they feel during play, the interaction with other children and the challenge the configuration of events provides (see Figure 7.1). The teachers enjoy the enthusiasm of the children and the ease of monitoring such a highly desirable activity in which so many can simultaneously participate. But, also of importance, the administrators, school board, and parents of the children in the school appreciate the fact that the structure provides the basis for learning; that in fact the teachers treat the structure as a learning station.

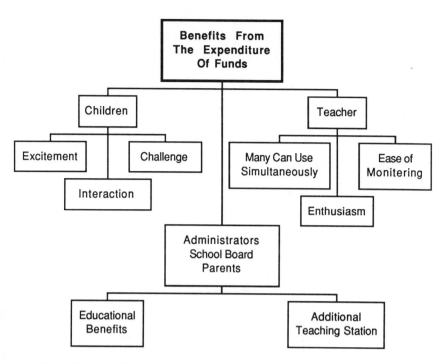

Figure 7.1 Benefits for children, teachers and administrators have been realized as a result of the Ysleta ISD purchase and installation

Project OLE` Curriculum

Ysleta became the first school district in the state of Texas which based a curriculum for an outdoor learning environment on the state mandated essential elements (Bruya & Sommerfeld, 1987). Further, Ysleta may be the first school district in the nation to organize an objective-based fitness and motor activity program which utilizes the playground as an outdoor learning environment.

The Ysleta teachers have available to them the materials needed to generate individualized problem solving activities for every child. The goal is to increase the learning of each student. As an additional benefit the Ysleta Independent School District children tend to feel better about themselves. They understand that they have the physical resources to solve movement problems and successfully meet physical challenges (see Figure 7.2).

For those who excel, enrichment activites are provided. These are designed to enhance problem solving and creative thinking skills (Alvarez, Hernandez, Jamison, Merez & Robinson, 1987). Children who successfully complete initial activities may be asked to find several different ways to climb up a ladder, or go over the net. Or, the teacher may toss a ball to a child coming down the slide and ask them to determine the number of different movements needed to complete the task.

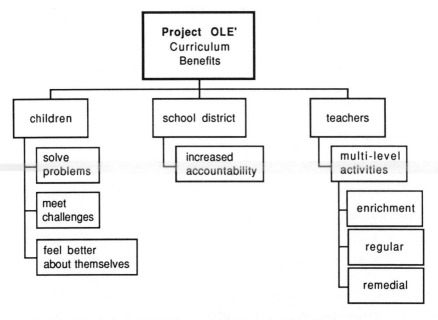

Figure. 7.2 The Project OLE' curriculum provides benefits for the school district, the children and the teachers.

Remedial activities are also suggested in the curriculum guide for those who are unable to perform well on the initial activities.

Examples include pull-ups which are modified by use of a low turning bar for a horizontal pull-up station prior to completing one regular pull-up (see figure 7.3). Basically, the activities include cooperative behaviors between children, and at the same time help initiate motor skill development in what is designed to be a supportive and pressure-free environment. The curriculum is designed to include activities in which students are able to work at their own level and pace, and which have multiple correct answers.

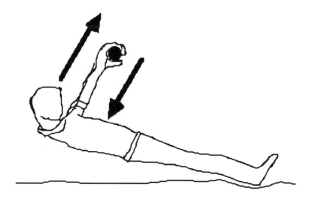

Figure 7.3 Remedial activities are designed to be similiar in requirement but of a lesser demand on the student than those thought to be regular, e.g. a modified pull-up as pictured is considered remedial while a vertical pull-up is considered regular.

Conclusion

Now a long and productive process to improve the facilities and the curriculum for the playground within the school district has resulted in both the environment needed to support the development of the child, as well as a curriculum which will insure that the activities used within the environment support positive growth. The next stage of curriculum development will likely focus on the interactions between uses of singular events within the structure, and on sequences of activities which place intricate and systematic demands on cognitive functioning (see Figure 7.4). This demand will center on the need for organizing the use of motor patterns to accomplish tasks (Kirchner, Cunningham and Warrell, 1970; Gabbard, LaBlanc and Lowy, 1987). In addition, expanded curriculum may also include the integration of math, science, social studies and other curriculum areas with motor activities as they relate to the outdoor learning environment (see Chapter 6).

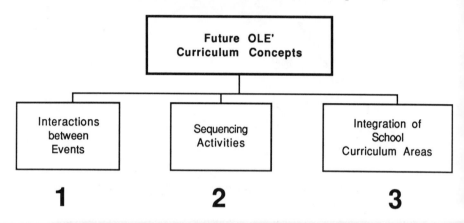

Figure 7.4 Additional curriculum concepts destined to be development for the Project OLE' structures on the Ysleta ISD playgrounds include increased integration and problem solving.

The school district is proud of its commitment to a unique instructional program of exceptional quality. It signals a significant investment of time, money and resources. It is an example of the potential development which can be realized in all schools.

Bibliography

Alvarez, R., Hernandez, T., Jamison, J., Meraz, D. & Robinson, B. (August,1987). Instructional strategies. El Paso, Tx: Bilingual Education Department, Compensatory Education Department & Elementary Education Department, Ysleta Independent School District.

Beckwith, J. (1985). Equipment selection criteria for modern playgrounds . In J.L. Frost & S. Sunderlin (Eds.), When Children Play. Wheaton, MD: Association for Childhood Education International, pp. 209-214.

Bruya, L. D. (1985). Design characteristics used in playgrounds for children. In J.L. Frost & S. Sunderlin (Eds.), When Children Play. Wheaton, MD: Association for Childhood Education International, pp. 215-219.

Bruya, L. D. & Buchanan, H. E. (1979). Complexity in an outdoor play environment. In C. Gabbard (Ed.), Texas A&M conference on motor development and movement experiences of children. College Station, TX: Texas A&M Press.

Bruya L. D. & Sommerfeld, D. (Eds.). (1987). Project OLE': An essential elements curriculum for use in the outdoor learning environment. El Paso, TX: Ysleta Independent School District.

Dauer, V. P. & Pangrazi, R. P. (1986). Dynamic physical education for elementary school children (8th edition). Minneapolis, MN: Burgess.

Frost, J. L. & Klein, B. L. (1979). Children's play and playgrounds. Boston: Allyn and Bacon Inc.

Gabbard, C., LeBlanc, E. & Lowy, S. (1987). Physical education for children: Building the foundation. Englewood Cliffs, NJ: Prentice-Hall, Inc.

Kirchner, G. (1985). Physical education for elementary school children (6th edition). Dubuque, IA: Wm C. Brown Co. Pub.

175

Kirchner, G., Cunningham, J. & Warrell, E. (1970). Introduction to movement education. Dubuque, IA: Wm C. Brown Co. Pub.

Logsdon, B. J., Barrett, K. R., Broer, M. R., McGee, R., Ammons, M., Halverson, L. E., and Roberton, M. A. (1984). Physical education for children (2nd edition). Philadelphia, PA: Lea & Febiger.

Shaw, L. G. (1976). The playground: The child's creative learning spaces (MH20743-034A1). Gainesville, FL: The Bureau of Research, College of Architecture, University of Florida.

CHAPTER 8

LEGEPLADS OF ARHUS
A 'PLAYSPACE' CONCEPT FROM
DENMARK

by

Sharyl Green
Landscape Architect, Playground Consultant,
and
Teacher of Young Children

In the heart of Denmark lies Arhus, a bustling industrial city of 250,000 people. Thousands of those people are children which city planners have chosen to recognize that in quite a substantial way.

In 1971, Arhus city planners, parks and recreation personnel including landscape architects and teachers, met to discuss the existing play opportunities for children in the city. It was recognized that: 1) many children were being raised by single parents, and 2) in many two parent families both parents were working. Child care needs had increased and included both pre-schoolers and school age children. This planning team felt that the city should be responsible for developing spaces where children could feel free to go without having to register ahead of time, show up on a regular basis, or pay admission. Further these spaces should be community based or located, available year around, and provide opportunities for creative activities both indoors and outdoors (Iverson & Daugbjerg, 1981).

The First Legeplads (playplace)

With this concept firmly in mind, the first legeplads (literally 'playplace') opened in 1971. There are now sixteen legeplads (pronounced "lie'-uh-plass") in Arhus with more on the drawing boards. The goal is to create a legeplads in each residential area that houses 800 to 1200 children, ages 0 to 14 years. Most legeplads currently serve neighborhoods with single family homes and high rise or multi-family developments. This mix is considered to be healthy for continuation of the 'playplace' concept.

Much of the success of the legeplads can be attributed to Anders Birch Iverson and Jens Ole Daugbjerg. Both were members of the original planning team. Since then, Anders has directed the planning and programming of the legeplads through the Recreation and Culture Administration of the city of Arhus. He works closely with the 16 playleaders and their assistants, as well as engaging in the planning process for new sites with Jens Ole Daugbjerg and other landscape architects employed by the City Parks Department. Each new plan must be submitted to the City Council for approval and funding (see figure 8.1).

At Bornenes Jord ("The Childrens Earth"), one of the oldest legeplads situated in the heart of the city, children are quick to jump off the tire swing and show visitors the details of the play yard. Walking through the sand play area under a huge old beech tree, three 9 year old children duck into a small shed and return grinning broadly with a hen apiece under their arms. Both children and hens seem at home with this arrangement. The parade moves on to the mesh enclosed outdoor home of the hens, where mothers of some of the infants and toddlers stand visiting, with one hand rocking the baby carriage and one eye watching in the direction of their youngsters at play.

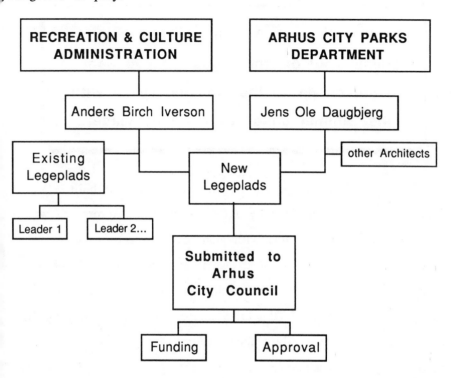

Figure 8.1 Arhus model for the development ot new Legeplads.

Chickens are scooted back to the coop and the parade moves on to the goat pen. A spry goat follows a child onto the roof of a small barn there. Feeding, petting and goat stories follow. The parade also passes a U-shaped design of 30 individual rabbit hutches situated on posts 2 feet off the ground. Each hutch is individually padlocked and a rabbit's name plate has been carefully placed above each door.

A large hand painted sign at the entry way to the hutches reads in Danish:

> **To the visitors: You must not take the animals out of the cages! If you want to get closer to the animals, speak with the "animal child" or the play leader.**

The visitors in the parade observe two small site-built playhouses on stilts connected by a flexible bridge. Across the way a large site-built climbing frame with giant cut out faces to walk through from one level to the next also is available. A circle of sitting stones defines the fire pit with scrap wood and branches nearby for burning. Inside the brick house (an indoor 'playplace'), the play leader moves easily among children engaged in a variety of art projects. He doesn't appear to be directing. Children have made choices and seem to be directing themselves. Here, the children-turned-guides leave the visitors and the parade loses its main attraction. No matter though, since adults are made welcome here by the leaders just as are all of the children.

Each legepads has a full time playleader who is on site 9:30 a.m. until 5:30 p.m. five days a week, year round. About half of the playleaders are men and half are women. The playleaders' union has negotiated for 2.5 assistants per site. These assistants are fully educated, by Danish standards, and are qualified for employment at ay care and youth work facilities. They also qualify for other professional positions which are responsible for working with children.

Although the tenure for an assistant may be short, the average tenure for a playleader is five years. Some have worked at the same site for as long as ten years (Anders Birch Iverson, personal communication while touring Legeplads, November 29, 1982). These playleaders and assistants are committed to the children of the neighborhood, and work closely with the parents of those children. These close ties are also part of the success story.

The 16 playleaders from the Arhus legeplads meet with Anders Iversen once a month to discuss budget and activities. The number of children at a site is recorded several times each day. Individual budgets for the legeplads are determined by the amount of use, based on these daily logs. Money is allocated for salaries, materials and toys, and maintenance of buildings and outdoor areas.

A visit to Vidtskue Vej (place with a distant view) under construction in early 1982 and later completed in the same year, reveals the careful site planning and detailing that goes into the development of each legeplads. Grading details have been staked and new plant materials are almost exclusively orchard trees and berry bushes that will be harvested by the children (see Figure 8.2).

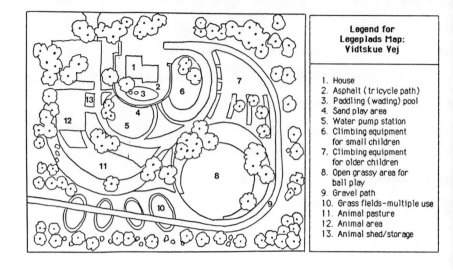

Legend for
Legeplads Map:
Vidtskue Vej

1. House
2. Asphalt (tricycle path)
3. Paddling (wading) pool
4. Sand play area
5. Water pump station
6. Climbing equipment
   for small children
7. Climbing equipment
   for older children
8. Open grassy area for
   ball play
9. Gravel path
10. Grass fields-multiple use
11. Animal pasture
12. Animal area
13. Animal shed/storage

Figure 8.2   The overview map of the Vidskue Vej Legeplads
demonstrates the richness and multivaried uses of the spaces.

Iverson talks about the soppebassin (paddling pool) that is being built near the new house (Anders Birch Iverson, personal communication while touring Legeplads, November 29, 1982). It is oval in shape (42' x 16') sloping to about 18 inches deep at its center Two large rocks are set into the asphalt surface. One of the rocks has a hole in the top, half an inch in diameter. Jens Ole Daugbjerg has designed a pumping system that allows the playleader to throw a switch inside the house that controls slow filling of the paddling pool (Jens Ole Daugbjerg, personal communication while touring Legeplads, November 24, 1982 and September 6, 1984). The water is piped from the city drinking water supply. The water is fresh each day and contains no added chlorine.

At the end of the day, the same switch drains the pool, so there should never be standing water on site after the leaders depart. The legeplads are not fenced except for the animal pens, so children do have access to the legeplads in the evening. However, the water is drained, and the animals are locked into their sheds overnight.

Pre-school children and accompanying adults play and lounge near the paddling pool. Children play in the nearby sand area, mainly engaged with a water and sand experimenting station .

A manufactured item from Sweden, this structure functions best if three or four children cooperate in its operation.

A pump handle and tank near the top, allow water to flow through a series of troughs. A paddle wheel, pulley system and water-stopping wooden plugs create interesting breaks along the path of the water. (As in the design of the paddling pool, the playleader is able to throw a switch in the house that controls the flow of water through this pump). The surrounding sand area is large enough to accommodate additional children digging, mixing and using a variety of toys. Two boys sit on the rocks along the edge quietly talking. One of them is stroking a rabbit on his lap.

Everywhere young children parade with wheeled vehicles. Some pull wagons behind. Others turn forward, backward, and rise up on the back two wheels of their four-wheeled moon cars. When the paddling pool is drained in the late afternoon, the gently sloped sides become a well used wheel course.

Pre-adolescents visit with the goat and sheep over the fence rail and collect chicken eggs that are taken into the house and stirred into the chocolate cake batter. Other children are creating special snack packs to be taken on Saturday to another legeplads where an all-city children's pet parade is planned.

Parents, caregivers, and babysitters are comfortable in this setting too. It is understood that pre-schoolers, toddlers and infants need to be accompanied by adults to the legeplads. School age children are free to come and go as they wish. The playleader is watchful, but not accountable for the whereabouts of given children.

Recently the Vidtskue Vej legeplads purchased a spinning wheel. Now city children witness most of the cycle from sheep to sweater by helping to raise the sheep, shearing them and then spinning the wool—all at the legeplads. The intention is to develop confidence in basic life skills as well as provide broad opportunities for experimentation . As a coincidental compliment the school curriculum includes a knitting class for all 9 year old children. Thus, the school and the legeplads combine resources to provide an understanding of the complete 'sheep-to-sweater' cycle.

The Legeplads - Playplace Concept

To develop a legeplads, Arhus-style, the following components are essential:

1. an outdoor site approximately 2-4 acres in size located within walking distance of residential areas;

2. a sturdy house (1200-1400 square feet of indoor playplace) that can be used year round; it should include a kitchen, workshop, bathrooms, work tables, office, and storage area;

3. edible fruit-bearing landscape and shade trees;

4. grazing areas and housing for sheep, goats, chickens, and rabbits;

5. sand and water play areas with apparatus;

6. fire pit and supply of scrap wood;

7. trikes, moon cars, wagons and secured storage area for these and other loose parts;

8. bike paths and loops;

9. climbing structures and other play apparatus for pre-school children;

10. climbing structures for school age children;

11. ball fields;

12. open grassy areas and cozy niches among the trees and shrubs;

13. picnic tables;

14. grassy bank and an outdoor threater space;

15. outdoor space with a good supply of materials for children's use when building their own structures;

16. the playleader who is trained, hired for full-time work, and involved in ongoing meetings for idea sharing and planning with other playleaders and an administrator (probably the most important component);

17. an administrator to be liaison to city officials, the playleaders, the community at large (this should be one who is astute in program planning and finances and is a public relations person extraordinaire).

The budget for an operation as extensive as the Danish legeplads would be considered large, although it is really fairly small when the advantages to the children are considered. For 14 of 16 legeplads in the Arhus area during 1984 approximately $854,000 was needed. Expenses were budgeted in 13 categories with wages for playleaders consuming the greatest proportion of the budget: 73%. The second largest budget item at 12% was the cost of play equipment and supplies. Other budget items included garden maintenance, telephone, vandalism repair, taxes and insurance, and others. Table 8.1 contains a complete breakdown on budget. The cost of a 'playplace' playground from inception to completion of construction reflects a great deal of planning time and effort. To develop Vidtskue Vej in 1982 the cost was approximately $220,000. That total included building the indoor play center or house on site (Anders Birch Iverson, personal communication while touring Legeplads, November 29, 1982).

Table 8.1 Budget items for a playground for children which is monitered by play leaders and includes a full sampling of play activities.

LEGEPLADS EXPENSE BREAKDOWN

Wages 73.0%

Play equipment and supplies 12.0%

Garden maintenance 3.0%

Telephone, etc. 3.0%

Buildings and fixtures 2.0%

Electricity, water, and heat 2.0%

Hired help 2.0%

Renovation 1.0%

Extraordinary maintenance 1.0%

Garbage removal 4%

Vandalism repair 3%

Work clothes allowance .2%

Taxes and insurance 1%

Although there are most certainly cultural and economic differences between Denmark and the United States, the idea of legeplads or 'playplaces' can be adapted here. There is a vast diversity of culture, lifestyle, and play settings in the United States just as in Denmark. So Americans must consider the problems of the United States and ask what can be learned and possibly applied from the Danish concept to school playgrounds.

The following concepts are a few of the major considerations that face developers of United States playgrounds. Discussion of each of these items centers on the unique arrangements made in Arhus, Denmark and the 'playplace' concept.

Vandalism

What is the worst incident of vandalism that has occured over the years at a legeplads? After thinking a minute Iverson told the story of a playleader arriving one morning to find all the locks on the rabbit hutches broken and all the rabbits missing. They were never found but soon after each rabbit was replaced with a new rabbit and to this day, the incident has never been repeated. Anders also mentioned that one night one of the houses was broken into, apparently just for play purposes. Basically, Anders reports that for the Arhus, Denmark legeplads, vandalism is almost an unknown problem. The reason, he says, is that the playleaders are doing a very good job in their efforts to make the children and the parents responsible for their own playground (Anders Birch Iverson, personal communication while touring Legeplads, November 29, 1982).

Safety

Anders also reported that the worst accident on an Arhus legeplads was the time a child broke an arm during a fall from a piece of climbing equipment (Anders Birch Iverson, personal communication while touring Legeplads, November 29, 1982). Since there are opportunities at legeplads for children to climb and move their bodies in all the ways they need to, falls of some sort are inevitable. But, children in Danish 'playplaces' don't have to use huge old swing frames like those found in the U.S. to try all of the gymnastics stunts children do. The structures there are more sanely designed with limited height given strong consideration.

191

Even more importantly, there is a wide variety of activities from which to choose in a legeplads. These include opportunities for children to rearrange and create, and to be active decision makers during their play.

Work

Children also participate regularly in real work at the legeplads. Feeding animals, cleaning their pens, using tools, planning special events, helping with repairs, cleaning up after themselves, and helping with younger children, are all part of their regular experience at the playplace. Children are done a disservice by assuming that most if not all of their play and recreation needs will be met by play equipment; even well designed equipment.

Observations of the legeplads in Denmark during summer and fall seasons revealed that children were most actively engaged and indeed spend a great deal of time with the care and feeding of animals. Experimentation during sand and water play, riding vehicles and working on creative activities in the house, including cooking and art projects, were the other biggest attractions. Climbing equipment appeared to be the least often used.

Conclusion

It is apparent in the legeplads that children become more responsible for their own safety and for the maintenance of their 'playplace' when they are expected to assume more responsibility in that environment. They need to have the opportunity to carry out real choices in environments that have been planned and designed to meet their needs.

Further, they must be able to count on consistent and creative adults to give them ongoing support in their work and play. Playleaders work alongside of children, helping them to carry out choices, and to improve skills. The day that snack packs were being prepared for a special event, there were as many adults as children helping with the task.

On rainy days, the children scurry to get the animals fed as the playleader uses a wheelbarrow to help speed the process. At the end of the chores there's a warm house to go into and the smell of fresh cake in the oven. "We're all in this together" is the message that rings clear again and again.

None of this could be happening if the city of Arhus had not approved a legeplads budget that allocates 73% of its funds to staffing the 'playplace' with qualified play leaders and their assistants. Remove them from the scene, and the success of the whole concept might collapse.

Iverson (personal communication while touring Legeplads, November 29, 1982) is convinced that the consistency that regular staff brings is extremely important. The concept would not be successful if there were a parade of volunteers to do the staffing. Someone needs to "own" the place, to see the work as his or her major focus, and be economically rewarded for their efforts. An 8-week summer recreation program run by college students who show up at the park 3 hours in the morning and 3 hours in the afternoon falls very much short of the playleader concept, in its most useful sense, as demonstrated at the Danish legeplads.

The playleaders on the legeplads in Arhus are role models. They are moving through their lives in ways children can appreciate, model and learn. In this type of environment there must be more than one child who has thought, "I want to be a playleader when I grow up."

The concept of legeplads as addressed in Arhus, Denmark signals an attitude change which is also needed here in the United States. The 'playplace' movement in Denmark indicates a concern for children and their welfare, beyond what is attempted in the United States.

The legeplads concept and the attitude which accompanies it has extended into other Arhus arenas for children as well. As an example of the concern for the whole-family concept of play, a list of other play sites for children and their families in the city of Arhus is provided:

1. school play yards;
2. infant, toddler, and pre-school child care center play yards;
3. after-school child care center play yards;
4. playgrounds outside the library and other public buildings;
5. playgrounds at housing developments;
6. playgrounds in single family neighborhoods;
7. backyard play areas;
8. municipal swimming pools;
9. municipal soccer fields;
10. an amusement park;

11. public parks and beaches;

12. enclosed public play areas for pre-schoolers on the ferry boats;

13. enclosed public play area for pre-schoolers at the international airport in Copenhagen;

14. paved bike paths throughout the city and surrounding towns.

Arhus is a city for the whole family! Perhaps the next generation of United States playgrounds will reflect those found in Arhus. Indeed, if this were the case, professionals everywhere would understand that our attitudes toward play and our children have changed.

Bibliography

Iverson, A. B. & Daugbjerg, J. O. (April, 1981). Play places in Arhus (Legepladser i Arhus). <u>Landscape</u> (<u>Landskab</u>), pp. 73-77.

CHAPTER 9

NEW CONCEPTS IN PLAYSTRUCTURES FROM THE COMMERCIAL SECTOR

by

Jay Beckwith
Play Structure Design Consultant

Twenty years ago the only way to create even marginally satisfactory play environments was to build them from scratch. One of the values of this process was its experimental nature. Over several years, many different materials and designs were explored. From this process a formula emerged which met the play needs for most schools in an economical and comparatively safe way.

The New Standard in Play Equipment

This formula, commercially introduced in 1975 as wooden structures by Big Toys®, has been widely accepted (see Figure 9.1). When translated into metal by Mexico Forge in 1980, the concept of the modular, linked playstructure became the industry-wide standard. Today, virtually every major manufacturer of play equipment has a version of this system (Landscape Structures, 1985; Iron Mountain Forge, 1987; Miracle, 1987).

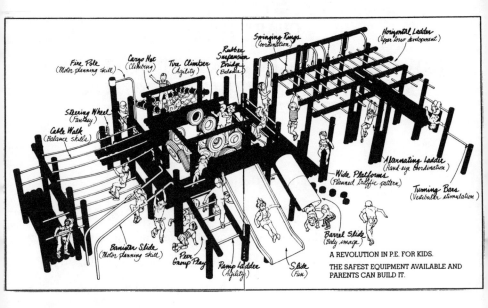

Fire Pole
(Motor planning skill)

Cargo Net
(Climbing)

Tire Climber
(Agility)

Rubber
Suspension
Bridge
(Balance)

Swinging Rings
(Coordination)

Horizontal Ladder
(Upper torso development)

Steering Wheel
(Fantasy)

Cable Walk
(Balance skills)

Alternating Ladder
(Hand-eye coordination)

Wide Platforms
(Planned traffic pattern)

Turning Bars
(Vestibular stimulation)

Banister Slide
(Motor planning skill)

Peer
Group Play

Ramp Ladder
(Agility)

Slide
(Fun)

Barrel Slide
(Body image)

A REVOLUTION IN P.E. FOR KIDS.
THE SAFEST EQUIPMENT AVAILABLE AND
PARENTS CAN BUILD IT.

FIGURE 9.1:

Schools now have a large range of play structure system
choices, all of which are of satisfactory quality. There is no longer
any reason for schools to be restricted to the pipe frame swings,
slides, and climbers of years gone by (see Bruya and Langendorfer,
in press, for a report on the structures currently in use).

Getting More for Less

Apparently one of the main reasons schools still buy antiquated, dangerous, and dysfunctional play equipment is based on the initial expense of the newer designs. A complex integrated structure can cost over $10,000 per school. The old swings and slides can be purchased for one-fourth that amount. It is easy for administrators who are strapped for funds to ignore the fact that the new designs: 1) can be used by greater numbers of children (see Chapter 3), 2) can provide additional development and learning benefits, 3) are easier to supervise, and 3) produce far fewer accidents.

Now, another factor must be considered by the administrator interested in establishing a new play structure on their school site. There has been a significant increase in the number of lawsuits initiated as a result of playground injury. Through awards to children and their parents, juries have been sending a strong message to schools (Adams, 1982; Mount, 1985; Toufexis, 1985; Weber; 1985). A new, higher standard of care is now becoming mandatory. Thus, most school districts have been forced to reconsider their traditional criteria when selecting new play equipment. The structures which are now available on the commercial market are better designed to provide developmental benefits as well as eliminate injury producing accidents.

Although budgets for playground equipment are increasing, they are still not lavish. Today when renovating playgrounds, schools seek to simultaneously increase benefits, provide for better supervision, and increase safety. However, manufacturers are not necessarily concerned with the same priorities. They know from past experience that certain 'price points' and features on a structure result in increased sales. Few manufacturers are concerned with producing products which are educationally sound. They may configure catalog designs to have, for example, a spiral slide, one standard slide, one overhead ladder, and a tire swing on a four-deck structure for under $8,000 to take advantage of normally desirable features and typical budgets. However, they may delete educationally important equipment such as turning bars, steering wheels, balance beams, fire poles, and other inexpensive accessories which significantly increase the positive benefits for the children provided by the structure. With these few additions a *good* play structure can be transformed into a *great* play environment.

To maximize the benefits of their purchasing dollars schools must take more control over the selection of play activities included on the playstructure. Administrators must consider how development can be supported through play experiences and challenges supported by play structures. They must look beyond price and manufacturer determined configurations to consider the details of the structure.

One of the greatest benefits of the new modular systems is that they can be readily modified to meet the specific goals of a school curriculum. With most systems it is possible to enhance the standard catalog designs and add less expensive "bells and whistles" that improve the play experience. With most products now on the commercial market even complete custom designs are possible. These systems are generally supported by the manufacturer with planning kits designed to serve purchasers as guides to the selection of appropriate options (Beckwith, 1979). In the use of a planning kit, an effort should be made to assess the play needs of the children who will use the structure, and determine the events which should be included.

In contrast to an orderly design process, nearly all schools take a hit-and-miss approach to playground improvement. Periodically, the P.T.A. or P.T.O. purchases another small piece of equipment to add to the playground. The selection process is generally the same; a few parents and staff get together over catalogs and buy one unit within their currently available budget. Unfortunately for the children, there is virtually no comprehensive planning or concerted effort to assess the overall needs of the children.

Schools might be better served, if instead of purchasing additional equipment with their current budget, they invested in professional assistance in the creation of a master plan. Such planning allows for the inclusion of details otherwise overlooked. These include such items as: 1) quiet play areas, 2) sheltered seating, 3) storage for loose parts, and 4) the programmed use of the structure.

Schools and P.T.O-P.T.A.s may not make such investments in professional assistance because they feel they will be throwing money away on plans which can never be realized. In fact, just the opposite is true. When schools develop environmental master plans they stand a much greater chance of gaining funding through an organized support process. Of course, it is also possible to waste money on the planning process. To avoid this circumstance the school should be careful to keep the cost of design assistance to around 10% — 15% of the total estimated project cost.

Whether funding comes from the school board, grants, private business, or an organized series of fund raisers, each benefits from the availability of a master plan. Indeed, it is the presentation of a master plan to communicate the educational and aesthetic qualities of the project which may prove to be pivotal to successful funding. The key elements of the planning process may prove to be documentation and presentation of: 1) a proper site analysis, 2) the assessment of educational needs, and 3) the benefits to be derived from play structure acquisition, 4) the finances necessary to accomplish the project, and 5) the overall design.

Generally master plans are implemented in phases over several years. This approach allows the school to initiate construction as funds are available. It is often the case however, even though the project is planned to span several years, that they are frequently implemented immediately. This occurs because the need is clearly articulated and thus, broadly supported. A well designed project, when presented with sufficient detail, creates the inertia needed to carry the plan through to early completion. This momentum will draw together all of the elements necessary to complete the project.

Future Solutions

During the next several years new options will become available for use on the playgrounds in the United States. Some of these options are discussed elsewhere in this document (see Chapter 1 for a discussion of Adventure Playgrounds; see Chapter 8 for a discussion of the Denmark Playground—Legaplads; see Chapter 7 for a discussion of an Independent School Districts' solution). Some designers within the United States have been busy attempting to provide new directions for playgrounds in our elementary schools. These include: 1) the addition of new challenging play events, 2) inclusion of elements to support development other than gross motor play, 3) the inclusion of loose parts in the play experience, and 4) the use of the play structure as a 'stage set' to expand classroom curriculum.

More Challenge. Since many adult concepts about playgrounds are based on personal experience of swings and slides, they tend to under estimate the value and importance of including innovative and challenging play apparatus in our structure designs. Indeed, the current liability trends tend to influence us to "sanitize" playground structures of all but the most familiar activities.

As an example, a well designed chain net climber was deleted by a well meaning safety committee and replaced with an arch climber. The basis for their decision was that children might fall through the net and onto the ground if it were included. The committee ignored the facts. The arch climber was actually higher and was thus capable of producing greater injury if a fall should occur. In addition, the arch climber was constructed of steel, increasing the likelihood of injury if a fall onto the climber should occur. The resultant design had two arch climbers and lacked a dynamic climbing challenge which the net climber would have provided.

The result of the misguided but well-intentioned decision was to produce a structure which reduced the degree of challenge with no additional assurance of improved safety. In addition, the net climber would have increased child interest in the structure because the structure would have provided greater variety of climbing experience needed for improvement of motor skill (Schimdt, 1977, 1982; Gabbard, LeBlanc and Lowy, 1987; McIntyre, Bruya, Eubank and Jackson, 1982).

Planning must proceed from fundamental curriculum goals which clearly set forth the specific benefits or challenges to be derived from each play event or piece of equipment. As far as possible these understandings should be based on empirical evidence; evidence which demonstrates the benefits of a piece of equipment as well as its safety. In addition, the planning process should reflect a concern for the overall mix of activities designed to provide graduated challenge. Only when this basic work is accomplished will innovative, safer, and truly challenging environments be possible on our elementary school playgrounds.

An example of an innovative play event which may better meet the need for equipment which provides greater challenge for stability and balance is replacement of playstructure decks with nets.

The nets increase the demand for balance and therefore increase challenge on the playground. In addition, replacing the solid decks with nets reduces running and games of chase and thus, improves safety as well. Nets also tend to produce more caution in younger children, since the visual awareness of height and perceived difficulty or challenge is increased.

Another example of a product which was developed in the attempt to meet curricular goals or assessed needs for graduated challenge was introduced in 1985 .   This system, called Kid Spaces™ (Iron Mountain Forge, 1987), was intended to create an environment which specificially attracted younger children. The scale and configuration of the Kid Spaces™ makes them unappealing to children six and older. Older children perceive them as ' too babyish, ' so they choose not to play on them. This is in distinct contrast to all former ' tot ' designs which were unsuccessful at exclusively meeting the specific needs and desired challenges of children six years and younger.

Future play equipment development must depend on a deeper understanding of children's needs and behaviors if they are to be successful. Through insights which result from such understanding, new products can be created. These in turn must be rigorously tested for safety.

However, the entire process from conception to production is relatively slow since the pace of innovation will ultimately be determined by the public's willingness to purchase and use innovative equipment. Unless new products are are presented as part of a rational educational agenda and clearly demonstrate their significant advantages, schools will continue to purchase inexpensive swings and slides. Thus, if products are to be accepted, manufacturers must clearly communicate the learning which can be gained from improved products and the developmental benefits which they embody.

Beyond Gross Motor Play. Our society is obsessed with competitive, rule structured, ball skill or sport types of play. This contention is easily supported be the fact that ball fields constitute approximately 97% of the available space on most school playgrounds. Play structures and equipment usually constitute less than 3% of the total play area. The total cost for installation and maintenance is even more disproportionate. However, this is not the case in quality early childhood education environments.

In early childhood education environments, play areas and play structures are generally built expressly to meet the needs of young children. The ratio of ball areas to play structure areas is more balanced and favors the use of play structures and equipment. Those who work closely with young children are keenly aware of their needs for a wide variety of play experiences, including dramatic play, social play, manipulative and constructive play. They understand that young children do not possess the social or motor skills necessary to successfully compete in sports. Therefore, in quality early childhood education environments, game spaces often occupy only a small part of the total area provided.

In contrast, most public schools ignore the fact that many of their students are developmentally not ready for sport. They provide large ball areas with only small amounts of space designated for play structures or other play experiences. As such, these play yards make only a minimal contribution to meeting the developmental needs of young children. For K-3 grade playgrounds the attempt to meet gross motor needs of these children consists almost entirely of traditional large apparatus of the type discribed in Crum & Eckert (1985) and in Where Our Children Play (Bruya & Langendorfer, In Press).

The National Survey of Elementary School Playgrounds establishes that most school playgrounds are only marginally functional and for the most part hazardous (Bruya & Langendorfer, In Press). Strong case can be made for playground renovation. It would be a shame however, to reconstitute the same fifty-year-old standard (Butler, 1958). Now is the time to create environments which provide for the total range all children's developmental needs.

Loose Parts. Only a small portion of the young child's learning is abstract and conceptual. The younger the child, the more that learning is a matter of touching, experimenting, and combining elements to extract information about the environment (Roberton and Halverson, 1984). For this reason, play environments which

207

include equipment which can be manipulated by children are far more appropriate than those in which all elements are fixed.

'Adventure Playgrounds' are partially based on the notion of loose parts. Thus, much has been made of 'Adventure Playgrounds' as a model for the future of American playgrounds (see Chapter 1 for a brief review of some of these arguements). In order to improve the acceptance of the loose part concept, educators must understand the reasons that the 'Adventure Playground' concept has not become the successful in the United States.

One basic element of the 'Adventure Playground' is the concept of a child constructed environment built from available loose part or scrap building materials. Several problems arise from this process, and these may be part of the reason that the 'Adventure Play' concept has never reached significant acceptance in the United States.

First, generally speaking, real construction skills, like nailing and sawing 2 x 4's, do not begin to emerge until the age of eight or nine years, making the program less valuable for young children but possibly appropriate for older elementary school children. Second, when children construct environments, a sense of ownership is created which is in conflict with the idea that public facilities are accessible to and essentially owned by all members of the community. Finally, the image of the adventure playground with its rickety constructed structures may offend casual adult observers as well as conjure up fears of accidents and lawsuits. While 'Adventure Playgrounds' may be conceptually correct, other types of loose parts systems must be developed if the idea is to gain wider acceptance.

A new loose parts playground product has been tested over the last five years. This product incorporates many of the same modular components as other products currently on the market but adds certain elements which can be manipulated by the children.

Several design considerations have become evident as this system has neared production. First, the parts must be very strong yet light enough for children to move easily. Second, they must connect simply enough for use by young children, and third, must avoid pinch points. These loose parts must also fasten securely enough to be safe. Finally, they must be durable and cost effective.

Basically, these technical difficulties have been overcome and the product will probably be available for use in the schools soon. Thus, it will be possible to begin to provide loose parts play on typical playgrounds with equipment not too different from structures which have already achieved market prominence. However, as loose parts products near commercial production, new issues have drawn into focus.

A lack of play leadership to insure safe handling and to supervise the use of loose parts on the playground makes the introduction of the product commercially questionable. Without play leaders to secure the distribution and collection of loose parts, the system may be impossible to implement in our school yard playgrounds in spite of the proven benefits for the growth of children.

In an attempt to overcome some of the problems associated with the lack of play leadership, loose parts will be supplied in a sturdy steel storage box and directed initially to early childhood education programs. This approach is being taken since early childhood educators more readily subscribe to the concepts of loose parts and play leadership. The long term goal is to gain acceptance for the notion of play with loose parts on our elementary school playgrounds. By beginning with early childhood programs, it is reasoned that its success will provide the understanding needed to make loose parts play a success in our elementary schools.

Programming and the Play Structure

"It ain't what you got . . . it's the way ya use it."

But, even without loose parts, existing modularly designed systems can be configured in ways which allow play leaders to improve the benefits of the equipment for children. For example, let's assume that several modular parts, which include gymnastic type apparatus, are selected for inclusion in a play structure .

Horizontal ladders, balance beams, and turning, climbing and parallel bars can be included in an existing linked structure. Thus, through careful planning, outdoor teaching stations can be created on the play structure. Including such teaching stations on the playground has the added benefit of providing the children with the opportunity for daily practice during recess.

Even without added features, most play structures can be used instructionally (Bruya & Sommerfeld, 1987; see Chapter 7 for a brief description of Project OLE'). What is needed is an attitude that learning does not stop at the classroom door and that physical education is more than learning sports; it includes all aspects of motor competence as well as safety.

Play for All

In September 1985, one hundred and thirty multi-disciplinary experts convened at Stanford University to address the problem of providing challenging and safe play environments for all children. Called The 'Play for All' Conference, the meeting was held to resolve the problems which arise in the consideration of the interrelated design concepts of accessibility, safety, and challenge. It was determined that these concepts must be considered simultaneously. This results in environments which more adequately meet the needs of all children.

One example of unbalanced emphasis on only one aspect - accessibility - is the inclusion of a ramp built to provide access for wheelchairs to the slides on play structures. If safety and challenge are not considered simultaneously with access, the ramp could be used as a bike challenge course and thus, make the safety of users doubtful. Following several days of intensive consideration of these variables the professionals attending concluded that many workable solutions already exist which could move us toward vastly improved play environments.

In addition to decisions about practical details for playgrounds, the conferees were united in their desire to see play leaders introduced into as many playgrounds as possible. They concurred that the introduction of play leaders is critical to the optimum beneficial use of playgrounds by all children. Other solutions are scheduled for publication in winter 1987-88 by the 'Play For All' organization.

Conclusion

As our society matures the 'wild places' for play become increasingly scarce. To develop the independence and flexibility of mind, body, and spirit which will be required of adults in the future, childhood experiences must be filled with exploration, discovery, and challenge. Creative play in enriched environments can be used as a powerful tool to develop flexible and open minded people.

Playgrounds designed to support all of the developmental needs of children are not just places where kids go to burn off energy. They can be important learning resources which will produce adults better able to cope with open ended options and choices. Unfortunately, the results of the AALR—COP Survey indicate that our elementary school play environments are being under-utilized in this regard.

The reassessment of the safety of playgrounds as demonstrated by the National Survey of Elementary School Playgrounds provides us with an ideal opportunity to improve the learning potential of these facilities. When play facilities are improved, it is also possible to redefine the need for play environment access and integration of children of all abilities.

With these priorities in mind, future playgrounds have the potential to be radically different, in both appearance and function. Maybe the Survey findings will mark the end of today's paved desert with pipe frame apparatus and initiate the dawn of a new era in playgrounds for all children.

Bibliography

Adams, S. H. (1985).   Court hits hard again with new liability twists. Athletic Purchasing and facilities, 6(5), 12—16.

Bayless, M. A. (1985, February).   A liability checklist.   JOPERD, 49.

Beckwith, J. (1979).   Playground planning and fund raising guide for schoolyard bigtoys.   Tacoma, WA: Northwest Design Products Inc.

Bruya, L. D. & Sommerfeld, D. (Eds.). (1987).   Project OLE': An Essential Elements Curriculum for Use with the Outdoor Learning Environment.   El Paso, TX: Ysleta Independent School District.

Bruya, L. D. & Langendorfer, S. J. (Eds.). (In Press).   Where our children play: Elementary school Playground Equipment. Washington, DC: AAHPERD, AALR-COP.

Butler, G. D. (1958).   Recreation areas: Their design and equipment (2nd ed.).   New York: The Ronald Press.

Crum, J. F., & Eckert, H. M. (1985).   Play patterns of primary school children.   In J. E. Clark & J. H. Humphrey (Eds.), Motor development: Current selected research (99-114).   Princeton, NJ: Princeton Book Club.

Gabbard, C., LeBlanc, E. & Lowy, S. (1987).   Physical education for children: Building the foundation.   Englewood Cliffs, NJ: Prentice-Hall, Inc.

Iron Mountain Forge (1987).   Kid Builders playground equipment. Farmington, MO: Author.

Landscape Structures (1985).   Landscape Structures/Mexico Forge: Play equipment, sports & fitness, site furnishings catalogue 1986/1987.   Delano, Mn: Landscape Structures Inc.

Miracle Recreation Equipment Co. (1986). Working hard for recreation: 1986 Catalog. Grinnell, IA: Author.

McIntyre, D., Bruya, L., Eubank, K. & Jackson, A. (1982). Gait characteristics of children during free ascent climbing performances. Human Movement Sciences, 1, 210-214.

Mount, C. (1985, January 15). Boy injured on slide gets $9.5 million. Chicago Tribune, p.1-section 1, p.1-section 2.

Roberton, M. A., & Halverson, L. E. (1984). Developing children-- Their changing movement. Philadelphia: Lea & Febiger.

Schmidt, R. A. (1982). Motor Control and learning. Champaign, IL: Human Kinetics.

Schmidt, R.A. (1977). Schema theory: Implications for movement education. Motor Skills: Theory into Practice, 2, 36—48.

Toufexis, A. (1985, March). No Mickey Mousing around. Time, (Law Section), 54.

Weber, J. (1985, November 19). An affordable need: Skyrocketing costs trigger anger alarm. Rocky Mountain News, p.1-B, p.14-B.

PART FOUR:

The School Playground And Risk

CHAPTER 10

A System to Manage The Risk of Lawsuit*

by

L. D. Bruya
North Texas State University

Jay Beckwith
Play Structure Design Consultant

Liability has become an issue for administrators who conduct programs and maintain facilities for the public (Bruya & Beckwith, 1985). Concern has spread to those who maintain and monitor playgrounds provided for use by the children of our nation (Wallach, 1985). Current trends in the insurance industry have also served to focus public attention on the question of liability (Eads & Ruete, 1984; Cohn, 1985; Hughes, 1985; Weber, 1985).

The Problem

With the publication of the United States Consumer Product Safety Commission report on playground equipment safety (Besson, 1979), and its recommendation for surface under structures to protect against the impact of falls (Hewes, 1974; Beckwith, 1979; Beckwith, 1983a; Beckwith 1985b; Bruya, 1985b; Witt, 1985), a national standard for playgrounds is being established. Although the USCPSC Guidelines (1980a,1980b) were intended

*Note: This manuscript is adapted from one published in Children's Environments Quarterly, Vol 2 Number 4, Winter 1985, by the same authors.

as suggestions, they have taken on the function of standards simply because no other higher level criteria have been available [1].

As a consequence of liability problems, administrators are becoming cognizant of the risks involved in providing and maintaining play spaces for children (Mount, 1985), while parents possess an increased awareness of legal options for redress of losses associated with injuries. It is now mandatory that administrators and professionals be concerned and conversant with these emerging standards.

A system is needed which will provide the necessary information and materials needed for training persons in their organizations to oversee safety and to train staff in record keeping procedures. These are the two most important components to reduce losses associated with injury on the playground. If documentation and record keeping are avoided it is difficult for the school district to defend itself.

Of course, one might imagine that the elimination of play equipment would solve future injury problems. However this approach leaves educators and administrators open to criticism. Part of administrative responsibility is to provide children a safe and stimulating environment in which children are more likely to learn. Since playgrounds cannot be eliminated, a system must be developed to protect school interests. The only real solution is the latter. We must move to establish a system to protect ourselves in a court of law should it become necessary.

In most cases where a lawsuit results from an injury sustained on the playground, negligent design and/or maintenance is alleged (Penman & Niccolai, 1985). This is true since data indicates that children will fall from the structure (Besson, 1979), whether the equipment is of the traditional separated format or of the contemporary linked unified format (Bruya, 1985c). In spite of improvements in safety railings (Beckwith, 1983b, p. 24; Iron Mountain Forge, 1985), ground cover materials (Reese Industries Inc., 1985), and recently the initiation of a new safety system using nets (Bruya, Sullivan, & Fowler, 1979), there will still be falls and the subsequent potential of lawsuit.

Precedent

If a recent court case settled for $6.3 million can be taken as a sign of the times, the courts are likely to interpret current laws governing the assignment of negligence in new ways. The Thompson case, in which the Seattle School District unsuccessfully defended itself against lawsuit, is a case in which this occurred (Adams, 1982; Adams & Bayless, 1982).

During a football practice, Chris Thompson tackled an opponent making contact first with his head, using what is called a "spear" tackle. During the execution of this manuever Chris severed his spinal cord and became a paraplegic. In an unprecedented move, the courts ruled in favor of Chris Thompson and his parents on the grounds that the school district and its employees failed to warn him or his parents adequately of the dangers involved in playing football.

In addition to failure to warn, the court determined that the district also failed to properly instruct. The school district also was determined to be negligent in the following areas: 1) failure to keep adequate injury reports, 2) failure to monitor injury reports, 3) failure to establish an officer in charge of safety in the school district, 4) failure to provide safety clinic training for its employees, 5) failure to develop a district wide policy towards safety, 6) failure to provide a curriculum or safety manual for its employees, and 7) failure of the school district to perform a regular evaluation of fields and equipment used. As these failures are considered, administrators should keep in mind that although the failures are specifically assigned to this case, legal precedent allows the Thompson-vs-Seattle case to be used in other applications. It could, for example, be applied to legal action related to accidents on the playground.

Precedent for the court decision against Seattle Public Schools apparently was based in an interpretation of the fourteenth amendment in which the right to due process is guaranteed. The decision in favor of Chris Thompson drew from court cases in which the right to procedural due process had been established (Kemerer & Deutsch, 1979). In effect, this means that the Seattle School District did not establish an adequate procedure to warn participants of inherent dangers.

Although an established procedure designed to insure the safety of its students would not have guaranteed that the Chris Thompson lawsuit or others like it would not have been filed, the likelihood of suffering an award of this magnitude would have been greatly reduced. To have any protection, however, a well documented support system used to systematically record the safeguards undertaken by the school district is required.

After a lengthy review and careful consideration of all phases of its program, the Seattle school district established a plan to prevent similar situations from occurring again (Chris Thompson, 1982; Seattle School District, 1984; Twardus, 1982; Warning Agreement, 1984). Part of that plan included a system of documentation designed to demonstrate safeguards the school district would undertake in the attempt to competently and professionally address the issue of safety.

The district designed a nine point system of checks and balances. These provisions included the following: 1) develop a form for parental signature which indicates assumption of risk [this included a detailed description of possible injuries that might occur as a result of participation], 2) establish procedures and criteria for the selection of supervisory personnel, 3) establish a process of continuous education for its supervisors, 4) develop a system of site assessments which includes program leaders, equipment, and facilities, 5) develop curriculum and safety manuals for use by its personnel, 6) regularly update and keep available all published materials concerning liability and risk management, 7) establish and monitor a safety program, 8) maintain injury records to pinpoint potential problems, and 9) summarize in a yearly injury report, needed programmatic changes which will likely eliminate or reduce the future occurrence of injury (see Figure 10.1).

greatly reduced. To have any protection, however, a well documented support system used to systematically record the safeguards undertaken by the school district is required.

After a lengthy review and careful consideration of all phases of its program, the Seattle school district established a plan to prevent similar situations from occurring again (Chris Thompson, 1982; Seattle School District, 1984; Twardus, 1982; Warning Agreement, 1984). Part of that plan included a system of documentation designed to demonstrate safeguards the school district would undertake in the attempt to competently and professionally address the issue of safety.

The district designed a nine point system of checks and balances. These provisions included the following: 1) develop a form for parental signature which indicates assumption of risk [this included a detailed description of possible injuries that might occur as a result of participation], 2) establish procedures and criteria for the selection of supervisory personnel, 3) establish a process of continuous education for its supervisors, 4) develop a system of site assessments which includes program leaders, equipment, and facilities, 5) develop curriculum and safety manuals for use by its personnel, 6) regularly update and keep available all published materials concerning liability and risk management, 7) establish and monitor a safety program, 8) maintain injury records to pinpoint potential problems, and 9) summarize in a yearly injury report, needed programmatic changes which will likely eliminate or reduce the future occurrence of injury (see Figure 10.1).

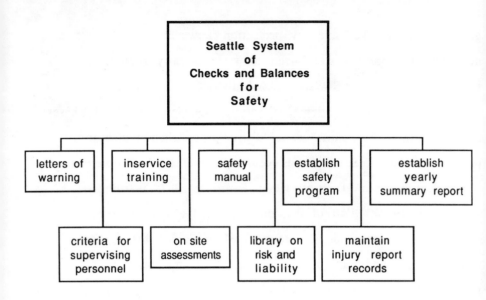

Figure 10.1 The Seattle documentation system was designed to record and file all pertinent information related to safety.

The Athletic Director of the Seattle Public Schools indicated that, "What the Thompson case did was approach safety from a different angle—advising the athlete of the risk involved" (Youth Sports, 1984). What before was thought to be self-evident and assumed risk now must be outlined for the player and the parents. Although it is certain that some injuries will occur in the future even with the newly established system of safety checks and balances, the real difference for the Seattle School District will be that they have the system to back them up. They will be able to demonstrate a systematic attempt to protect and warn players of the risks involved.

A Working System on the Playground

A risk management process must be developed for playground facilities to satisfy the same purpose as that recognized by the athletic department of the Seattle Public Schools. Although difficult and time consuming time to establish, a documentation system will be worth the problems when the district is called to defend itself.

The real benefit of the initiation of any safety program and its documentation process is locating and removing problems on playgrounds in order to prevent injuries and lawsuits. A brief explanation of a safety check system is provided below and can be used to provide a measure of protection for both the school district administrators of the playground and the children who use it.

Warning Letters and Signs. In the case of elementary schools and the playground facility, a letter warning of the specific danger of injuries which might be suffered during play should be sent home for signature. Parents may refuse to sign. To avoid this problem it is better to include the following in the letter:

"Although my signature does not constitute a release of the school from the responsibility of caring well for my child during school hours, my signature signifies that I have read the letter and understand the risks involved for my child on the playground" (see Figure 10.2).

Thus, Parents are alerted to the potential for injury and the school district is aware that special arrangements may need to be taken.

It should be noted that sending a letter home from school does little to solve the problem of warning players who use school playgrounds after hours. The question of warning presents a different challenge. How can administrators of playground facilities insure that adequate warning is provided for those players who use free access playgrounds with or without parental guidance?

Marguerite Giesa Elementary School
Mt. Clement School District
Clement, Washington

Dear Parents:

This is to indicate that participation in some play activities may result in injury - some may even be severe. Although every precaution to protect your childs' safety has been taken, reports by the US Consumer Product Safety Commission suggest that children will fall from equipment on the playground during normal exploration and play. Although a safety absorbtion surface has been provided by the school district to protect your child from severe injury during these falls it is possible that injury may still occur. These injuries include broken bones, damage to internal organs, and very rarely, death.

If you have questions concerning the safety process the school district is providing please call the school safety officer, Mr. Johnson, at 847-9387 or the school principal at Samuel Morris elementary school, Ms. Herrickson. The school number is 847-6322.

Please detach the signed note and return it to the school for our file.

Towards a Safer School Playground,

Anne Herrikson

Anne Herrickson, Principal
Marguerite Giesa Elementary School

- -

Although my signature does not constitute a release of the school from the responsibility of caring well for my child during school hours, my signature indicates that I have read the safety letter and understand the risks involved for my child on the playground.

signature *Susan & Henry Titleson*   date *9/14/3*

parents' name *Susan & Henry Titleson*
please print

Figure 10.2   The letter sent home to parents, insures that they are aware of potential injury which could occur on the playground.

Signs, placed on the playground in readily observable places, can be used to good effect. This procedure establishes a warning system in the absence of supervision for at least those parents and children who are able to read or understand graphics (Galvan, 1985).

Criteria for the signs should include a statement of caution and a thorough description of injuries which might occur. An example of a signs which players and their parents might see upon entering the playground is shown in Figure 10.3.

For those unable to read or who do not read English, all warning signs should carry a graphic display of content. Figure 10.3 demonstrates a graphic sign which might be used to warn non-reading players that they should not run. Additional signs in the form of smaller pictograms could be posted on the structure itself. These would provide warning for children just prior to use of the event or describe the level of challenge the event provides. While these forms of signage would not constitute a total public awareness program, the effort, care, and concern, plus subsequent documentation recorded and filed, can be used to demonstrate a competent attempt to provide adequate warning.

CAUTION
Possible injury may occur during play on the playground.
Avoid lifting or placing children on the structure in a position in which they feel uncomfortable. If they can't do it on their own they are not ready to do it.
<u>Possible Severe Injuries from Falls</u> 1. Blows to the head 2. Broken bones 3. Neck or spinal injury 4. loss of teeth, concussions   severe bruises, tissue injury

Figure 10.3 Signs on the playground can provide written and graphic warnings to players.

Inspection.   Another technique to insure safety on the playground may well become law in Chicago.   This is the result of a recent case in which a child was hurt when he fell from a slide (Mount, 1985).   In a proposed ordinance, to be placed before the voters, all playgrounds would be subject to annual safety inspections (Galvan, 1985).

The problem with a system of inspection as proposed (Witt, 1985) is that once-a-year may not be nearly often enough in a school district with heavy use and/or significant vandalism.   Witt suggests inspections on a weekly or even daily schedule.   Although the benefits of an inspection program are fairly self-evident, the time table for such observations must be established relative to the needs of the district.   The intensity of use, or even the uniquenesses of a particular structure, should be used to establish an administrative · schedule for structure safety review.

The instrument used to assess the play environments also is important.   An inspection instrument, can be used in regular evaluations of the play structure (Bruya, 1985a; 1985d).   This instrument should be divided into sections and should be similiar in content to the instrument used to generate data for the National Survey of Elementary School Playground Equipment (Bruya & Langendorfer, in press).

The overall safety of the play equipment can be assessed using the answers questions to questions listed on the instrument, and provide accurate record keeping to help pinpoint problems (Youth

Sports, 1984). Kept in a file, these assessments are invaluable in proving that regular checks of all equipment have been made. This fact is of particular importance since *documentation is essential* for proper risk management (Adams & Bayless, 1982).

Documentation. A documentation system that can withstand the rigors of court scrutiny must be more inclusive than simply maintaining inspection files. The documentation process should be extensive and record decisions made from the start of planning for the school playground and its structures. Basically, a risk management documentation system, designed to withstand court critique, should include at a minimum the following six procedures: 1) design; 2) purchasing; 3) installation; 4) maintenance; 5) repair; and 6) the safety program (see Figure 10.4).

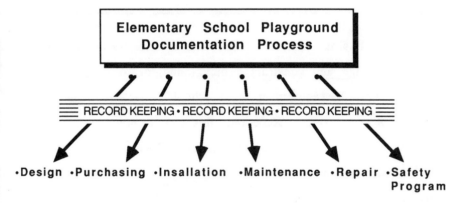

Figure 10.4. The system used in the elementary school to document procedures related to the playground include six processes

The Design Process. The first documentation step is to record and file information concerning the design process. Reasonable answers to three questions should be recorded, filed and available for review. The questions concern the designer, the parameters upon which the design is based and a rational for safety (see Table 10.1). Records kept concerning thoughts and rationale for these questions provide important documentation of the initial planning phases. The records will prove that all possible attempts have been made to select the safest and most advantageous design for a play structure which supports the growth and development of children.

Table 10.1   Answers to at least four questions are necessary during the process of designing a play structure for the elementary school.

Design Process Questions

Q1. What are the qualifications of the designer?
Q2. What are the parameters by which the design is to be evaluated?
Q3. Can proof of adherrence to the design parameters be provided?
Q4. What is the rationale for the design of safety on the structure?

The Purchasing Phase. Usually the decision to contract a consultant to design and construct a playground, or to purchase commercially available equipment for a school district, is made by the director of purchasing. Sometimes this task is completed with the recommendation of supporting personnel. Documentation of this part of the decision answers the question, *who made the decision to purchase a particular structure?*

It would also be advisable to ask for an opinion from other designers in the field. These opinions should be written and kept on file. Questions specifically addressed by the consulting expert include both strong points of the chosen structure, which are likely to support the growth and development of the child and weak points of the structure related to safety and potential risks (see Figure 10.5). Referenced sources should be included in the consulting expert's report. Although this service will add expense to the overall price of structures used for children's play, the potential support of the expert witness in court and the fact that input was sought at the beginning of the purchasing process is valuable.

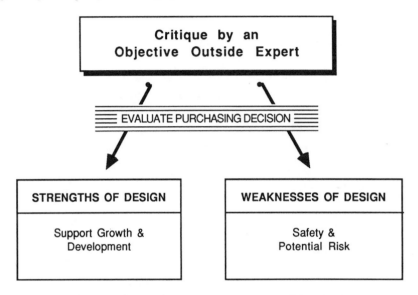

Figure 10.5   An outside consultant can provide a validity check for the chosen design, and strengthen the confidence associated with the decision to purchase.

The second purchasing process checkpoint documents the question, *how was the decision made?*   By inserting a design review phase, where interested parents and educators are invited to view the designs of the proposed structure (Beckwith, 1982), input and critique from concerned parties can be documented and recorded (Bayless & Adams, 1985).   At this point it would be wise to ask the sales agent supplying the equipment to be on hand to answer questions that might arise during the review. In addition to written minutes, questions concerning the safety of the structure should be compiled and answered in writing, by the sales agent, to provide further documentation.

A procedure to record those who attend such a meeting would add further evidence that a meeting was held and that some of the community was present. All papers which record the processes leading to decisions for purchase should be filed and retained in permanent storage.

The Installation Process. Installation should be carried out by a reputable contractor with the experience necessary to increase the likelihood of proper installation. No matter who is chosen, carefully document the question, *who installed the equipment?* It is advisable to select a well established construction firm over an unknown one, even though the company may not be the lowest bidder, since a defense is stronger if the installer is still in business, when legal questions arise.

The installation processes must be guided by specifications provided by the manufacturer. A record of *what were the specifications for installation?* will be important in later discussions to insure that proper criteria and procedures were established at the outset of the installation. The experience of the installer can be important since directions and/or blueprints must be understood by those responsible for installation. All of this material plus the installation manual should be kept as a permanent record.

Another documentation process begins at this time. It includes constant and regular monitoring of inspections. The intention the inspection process is to assure that proper procedurses were followed. Thus, it is extremely important that the school district can answer affirmatively when asked *whether records were kept of each inspection.*

Establishing proper playground inspection will take time and effort. All personnel should be provided with training to insure proper and uniform inspection. This is paticularly important in the case of larger school systems which may require multiple inspectors. A training seminar for inspectors should be conducted by someone outside of the installation process to insure lack of conflict of interest. While several functions will be performed during the inspection, it should keep as its focus the *adherence to the provided specifications.*

If specifications are at any point felt to be unreasonable or inadequate, then proper recorded documentation must be kept of *changes made in specifications* by whom and why were they made? But never undertake changes on your own (Beckwith, 1983b, p. 26). These changes must be agreed to in writing by the equipment supplier with all copies of change orders kept on permanent file.

At the conclusion of the installation and inspection process, a sign-off procedure is recommended. Suggestions for this process include co-signatures by the equipment supplier representative, the contractor in charge of installation and the project administrator, as well as the person(s) in charge of inspection. It is important that the installation process be entirely complete prior to signature. You should be prepared to answer the question, *what was the process for "signing-off" on the installation?*

The Maintenance Process. At this point a very real shift in accountability occurs. From now on, an adequate defense will rest on maintenance procedures. The manufacturer should provide a suggested maintenance schedule, and that schedule should be adhered to closely. This schedule is the first step in answering the question, *is a regular maintenance schedule planned?* The schedule, plus an office procedure to insure regular adherence by an assigned safety officer, helps establish *the procedure for insuring maintenance.* While a general schedule (i.e., "once a month") is appropriate, it is best not to designate a specific date since this may present problems later should the inspection occur at a different time.

The Repair Process. If during a routinely scheduled maintenance check problems are detected, it is important to establish and document a procedure for solving the maintenance problem. The report of maintenance problems should be dealt with immediately. The safety inspection officer or other designate should draft work orders as part of the reporting procedure. At this point, all dated work orders should be copied and filed.

The work order process initiates what is sometimes referred to as the problems procedure. As indicated in the previous paragraph, the inspection officer is the likely choice for recording when and *who initiates the maintenance procedure?* Once instructions for maintenance have been cut, it is extremely important that the actual labor for maintenance be provided promptly by a crew who is specifically trained to repair the structure. This provides the necessary answer to the question *is there a trained crew assigned to maintenance?* Not only should the crew and the task be identified in the documentaton, but the time of the work order request and the completion of repair should also be noted.

Upon repair, the question of *a maintenance follow-up process* becomes important. The follow-up process insures that repairs, once made, do not quickly become problems again. For example, weekly checks for the four weeks immediately following a repair should be made, and documentation of this fact recorded in the file. Following this once a week recheck process there should follow at least two bimonthly rechecks. Adhering to a problem identification program as suggested, insures that problems do not reoccur and that full responsibility for repairs has been accepted and demonstrated by the sponsoring agent. Following this recheck process a *return to a regular inspection schedule* can be made.

The Safety Program Process. In addition, a careful preparation of activities designed to establish safety on the playground should also be presented to the children prior to use of the equipment and at regularly scheduled intervals throughout the school year, with records of these sessions kept in the files.

Caring but Tough Response

Due to the recent court ruling in the case of Chris Thompson vs. Seattle Public Schools, it is evident that procedural risk management as outlined above, is now required to increase protection from loss due to an injury damage suit. Establishing a comprehensive program does not insure that suits will not be filed. Instead, the process provides the necessary material to show competence, demonstrate responsibility, and avoid large awards for plantiffs. Hopefully, the process will result in safer play equipment on which fewer children are injured, as well.

Recently there have been indications that the risk management process outlined above will provide an adequate defense. In the law section of <u>Time</u> magazine in March 1985, Toufexis reported that Walt Disney Productions had a successful program. It reinforces the need for documentaton, as well as demonstrating real caring for those injured while using Disney facilities. The *first contact with an injured party is made by a supervisor and security host* who is summoned immediately (see Figure 10.6). These persons interview all available witnesses as well as the injured party. Frequently, during this time, the parties involved say things that later demonstrate that Disney may not have been at fault. Comments like "I wasn't looking where I was going" or "It was my own fault" are recorded immediately following the incident.

Another technique employed by Disney is a long term evaluation and record system not unlike the regular assessment system for play structures mentioned at the beginning of this chapter (see Figure 10.6). Using a regular check-up technique, Disney was able to avoid a court ruling in a recent case against it, because their tree expert and his records for each tree indicated a regular maintenance check-up and recorded proper pruning. Thus, the fact that a branch fell and hurt a patron was determined to be a natural event rather than the result of negligence on the part of the Disney organization.

As an additional strategy to the **immediate attention** and **long term records techniques** that the Disney people use, they also encourage on-site visitation, as a part of their courtroom presentation. This personalizes, for the jury, Disney's high standard of maintenance. Disney also takes pains to enlist the support of the city leaders and the surrounding community itself. Although a school is not exactly in the same situation as a Disney World, it does provide a successful model. General public support and on-site visits are an important tool in reducing exposure to losses. This is a good example of the value of public review of purchases, to build support, as outlined earlier.

The final, and apparently pivotal Disney defense posture, is the willingness *to take a tough stand and go to court.* With a defense built on the concepts detailed here, and the willingness to trust in preparation and competency, hard work pays off (see Figure 10.6).

The Disney System Applied To The Schools

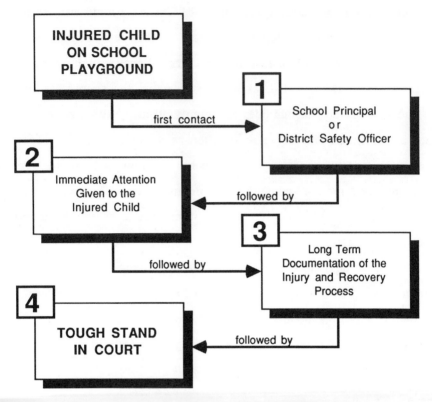

Figure 10.6   The Walt Disney Productions process for handling injuries could serve as a model for school systems.

Conclusion

It is apparent that the simple provision of equipment for children's play is no longer adequate. It is now necessary that procedures be created for performing and recording all aspects of the process of creating and maintaining schoolyard facilities; and for providing supervision of these structures for the purpose of meeting the needs of all children (Beckwith, 1985a). This insures the safety of the player and the solvency of the agency which provides the environment. It seems evident from current court decisions, that increased accountability will continue to be important.

End Notes

1. The PLAE Inc, Manuscript suggesting a more extensive list of playground guidelines is now in press.

Bibliography

Adams, S. H. (1982). Court hits hard again with new liability twists. Athletic Purchasing and Facilities, 6(5), 12-16.

Adams, S. H., & Bayless, M. A. (1982). How the Seattle decision affects liability and you. Athletic Purchasing and Facilities, 6(7), 12-16.

Bayless, M. A., & Adams, S. H. (1985, February). A liability checklist. JOPERD, p. 49.

Beckwith, J. (1979, January). You can build a playground. American School & University, pp. 28-31.

Beckwith, J. (1982, September). It's time for creative play. Parks & Recreation, pp. 37-42.

Beckwith, J. (1983a). Further thouhts on falling. ProData, 1(2), 3.

Beckwith, J. (1983b, May). Playgrounds for the twenty-first century. Cities & Villages, 21(5), pp. 22-26.

Beckwith, J. (1985a, May/June). Play environments for all children. JOPERD, pp. 32-35.

Beckwith, J. (1985b). Equipment selection criteria for modern playgrounds. In J. L. Frost and S. Sunderlin (Eds.), When children play (pp. 209-214). Wheaton, MD: Association for Childhood Education International.

Besson, E. H. (1979). Briefing memorandum: Public playground equipment. In the U. S. Consumer Product Safety Commission Report. Washington, D.C.: Consumer Product Safety Commission.

Bruya, L. D. (1985a, April). Comprehensive risk management for play environments. Paper presented to Illinois Parks and Recreation Association, Chicago, Illinois.

Bruya, L. D. (1985b). Design characteristics used in playgrounds for children. In J. L. Frost & S. Sunderland (Eds.), When children play (pp. 215-219). Wheaton, MD: Association for Childhood Education International.

Bruya, L. D. (1985c). The effect of play structure format differences on the play behavior of preschool children. In J. L. Frost & S. Sunderland (Eds.), When children play (pp. 115- 120) Wheaton, MD: Association for Childhood Education International.

Bruya, L. D. (1985d, April). A seminar on liability and risk management on the playground. Paper presented to Reese Industries, Chicago.

Bruya, L.D. & Beckwith, J. (Winter, 1985). Due Process: Reducing exposure to liability suits and the management of risk associated with the children's play area. Children's Environments Quarterly. 2, 4, pp. 29-35.

Bruya, L. D. & Langendorfer, S. J. (Eds.). (In Press). Where our children play: Elementary school Playground Equipment. Washington, DC: AAHPERD, AALR-COP.

Bruya, L. D., Sullivan, M., & Fowler, C. L. (1979). Safety on the horizontal ladder: An intermediate catch system. In C. Gabbard (Ed.), Texas A&M Conference on Motor Development and Movement Experiences of Children (pp. 10-12). College Station, TX: Texas A&M Press.

Chris Thompson vs. Seattle Public School District Case. (1982). Unpublished manuscript, Seattle Public Schools, Athletic Department, Seattle.

Cohn, D. (1985, November 29). Fairfax bans new wooden playgrounds. Washington Post, pp. B1, B7.

Eads, G., & Rueter, P. (1984). Designing safer products: Corporate responses to product liability law and regulation (product liability and insurance). Journal of Products Liability, 2, 289-291.

Galvan, M. (1985, January 31). Proposed ordinance aims to make playgrounds safer. Chicago Tribune, pp. 1, 9.

Herbstman, D. (1985, September 21). Personal communication.

Hewes, J. J. (1974). Build your own playground: A sourcebook of play structures, designs, and concepts from the work of Jay Beckwith. Boston: Houghton.

Hughes, P. R. (1985, December 6). Gripes over insurance soar to state record. San Francisco Chronicle, pp. 1, 4.

Iron Mountain Forge. (1985). Kid Builders Playground Equipment— catalog. Farmington, MO: Author.

Kemerer, F. R., & Deutsch, K. L. (1979). Constitutional rights and student life. St. Paul: West Publishing Co.

Mount, C. (1985, January 15). Boy injured on slide gets $9.5 million. Chicago Tribune, pp. 1-Sec. 1, 1-Sec. 2.

Penman, K. A., & Niccolai, F. R. (1985). Playing it safe. Designing sports facilities to avoid personal injury and litigation. American School & University, 57(8), pp. 36-38.

Reese Industries, Inc. (1985). Cushion Turf—advertising flyer. Chicago: Author.

Seattle School District Recommendations Based on the High Risk Study. (1984). Unpublished manuscript, Seattle Public Schools, Athletic Department, Seattle.

Toufexis, A. (1985, March). No Mickey Mousing around. Time (Law Section), p. 54.

Twardus, B. (1982). Seattle Public Schools memorandum: Safety guidelines. Unpublished manuscript, Seattle Public Schools, Athletic Department, Seattle.

U. S. Consumer Product Safety Commission (1980a). A handbook for public playground safety: Vol. I. General guidelines for new and existing playgrounds. Washington, D. C.: U. S. Government Printing Office.

U. S. Consumer Product Safety Commission (1980b). A handbook for public playground safety: Vol. II. Technical guidelines for equipment and surfacing. Washington, D. C.: U. S. Government Printing Office.

Wallach, F. (1985, October). Accidents, liability confront park staffs. American City & County, pp. 36-42.

Warning, Agreement to Obey Instructions, Release, Assumption of Risk, and Agreement to Hold harmless. (1984). Unpublished manuscript ? , Seattle Public Schools, Athletic Department, Seattle.

Weber, J. (1985, November 19). An unaffordable need: Skyrocketing costs trigger anger, alarm. Rocky Mountain News, pp. 1-BN,1 14-B.

Witt, H. (1985, January 16). Softer surfaces make suburban playgrounds safer. Chicago Tribune, p. 3-Sec. 2.

Youth sport injuries: Is the risk acceptable? (1984, January). Athletic Purchasing and Facilities, 8(1), 14-20.

DATE DUE

1/9/97			
APR 16 '02			
MAY 1 3 '02			
GAYLORD			PRINTED IN U.S.A.